Words of Grace

A Quick Reference Handbook for Christian
Leaders in Conducting Weddings, Funerals,
Baptisms, Worship Services, & Much More

Rev. Dr. Michael Morawski

Words of Grace

A Quick Reference Guide for Christian
Leaders in Conducting Weddings, Funerals,
Baptisms, Worship Services, & Much More

Rev. Dr. Michael Morawski

© 2016 Michael Morawski - Hartford, Connecticut USA

Printed in the United States of America

Unless otherwise indicated, Scripture references
are from the Holy Bible, New International Version
(NIV) Copyright © 1973, 1978, 1984, 2011
ISBN 978-0-692-57438-6

This book is dedicated to my fellow servants in the faith. . .

"It's the Holy Spirit's job to convict, God's job to judge, and my job to love."

— *Billy Graham*

"If you do what's right, you have nothing to fear."

— *Mike Morawski*

Table of Contents

✝

Preface..1
The Lordship of Christ...9
    The Other Ships......................................9
    The Names of God....................................15
The Call..17
Ministerial Ethics and Spiritual Protocol................27
    Principles of Conduct.................................27
    Protocol for Associate /Assistant Pastors..........29
    Guidelines for Detecting Negative Spirits........34
    The Six C's..36
Worship Services...44
    The Fall of Mankind Explained.....................44
    Why Worship?..45
    Jesus is the Answer....................................46
    Salvation Prayers......................................47
    Principles of Worship.................................48
    Worship Service Ideas................................50
    Appearance, Parking Attendants and Greeters....50
    Prayer of Invocation..................................53
    Hymns of Praise.......................................56
    The Purpose of Christian Music....................57
    Scripture Reading.....................................60
    Intercessory Prayer....................................64
    The Offering..65
    Offertory Prayers......................................66
    Benedictions..68
    Examples of Church Service Liturgies.............70
Baptism..77
    Water Baptism...77

    Water Baptism Services...................................80
    Step-by-Step: Full Immersion Baptism.............81
    Sample Baptism Service.................................85
    Baptism in the Holy Spirit..............................85
    The Seven Purposes of the Spirit Baptism........89
    Speaking in Tongues......................................91
    How Spiritual Power is Lost...........................94

The Lord's Supper/Communion............................95
    What It Is..95
    Emphasis on the Lord's Supper.......................97
    Preparation for Communion...........................97
    Sample Communion Prayer............................98
    Administering Communion............................99
    Communion at the Altar.................................99
    Suggested Communion Scriptures.................100

Weddings..105
    Guiding Principles of Marriage......................105
    Relationship Love Types................................109
    Wedding Guidelines Prior to Ceremony..........112
    Pre-Marital Counseling Journal......................115
    The Wedding Rehearsal.................................128
    Wedding Ceremony Positions........................132
    Formal Wedding Liturgy...............................133
    Formal Wedding Ceremony...........................134
    Informal Wedding Ceremony.........................139
    Informal Wedding Liturgy.............................140
    Renewal of Vows...141

Funerals..145
    Funeral Principles..145
    Guidelines for Performing a Funeral...............149
    Sample Funeral Liturgy.................................150
    The Funeral Service with Eulogy....................151
    At the Cemetery..156
    More Committal Examples............................159

Funeral Scriptures..161
Cremation..164
Dedications and Installations...............................167
Dedication of a Church Building....................168
Blessing a Home...170
Sample Home Blessing Prayer.........................171
Dedication of a Child or Baby........................171
The Commitment of the Parents.....................173
Installation Service for a Pastor/Leader...........177
Pastoral Counseling...179
What is Pastoral Counseling?.........................179
Guiding Principles..179
Cautions in Pastoral Counseling.....................181
Advantages of Pastoral Counseling.................182
Ten Key Realities of Pastoral Counseling.........184
Substance Abuse Counseling.........................188
Hospital and Home Visits...191
Visitation and Care Ministry Principles...........191
Modern Day Stressors...................................193
Visitation Benefits.......................................194
Other Hospital/Home Visit Guidelines...........195
Conflict Resolution...197
Conflict Resolution Process...........................199
Connecting Goes Beyond Words....................201
Correct with Love..203
How to Live In a Secular World............................205
Be Yourself, Be Real.....................................205
Remember To Whom You Belong..................208
Casting the Vision of Your Church........................211
Church Membership..215
Benefits of Becoming a Church Member.........216
Prayers for Certain Occasions...............................219
About the Author...226
Endnotes...227

Preface

Words of Grace is written exclusively to assist pastors, ministers and lay leaders in the performance of their clerical duties while serving our Lord Jesus.

Prayerfully, this helpful guide is presented with humility, dedication, love, accuracy, and faithfulness to God and His people. You can take this compact, easy to carry handbook wherever you go. It is designed to slip into your suit pocket, purse, or travel bag for instant access whenever the need arises. It guides you and your words through important topics during the many occasions and circumstances arising, sometimes at a moment's notice, in the life of a Christian minister or leader. It is also available in a Kindle version.

The topics covered herein are done so for the purpose of guiding you through specific presentations to a gathering of people in the Spirit of Christ. As such, each of these topics has a multitude of glorious, in-depth readings crafted by learned scholars down through the centuries. This book allows you to easily and effectively present the Gospel of Jesus Christ during life's most joyous and challenging situations and ceremonies.

Appropriate Scriptures, pertaining to the situation at hand, are placed in each section. This is meant to prevent awkwardly looking through the handbook or your Bible trying to locate them while standing before an observant crowd. Additional Scriptures, which you may prefer to read directly out of your own

Bible, are also included.

For those seeking deeper knowledge and guidance, an extensive list of excellent books is provided at the end of the book for more comprehensive study.

First and foremost, *Words of Grace* is a reminder that Christian leaders must always perform their duties with the utmost professionalism and care by the prompting and guidance of the Holy Spirit. The number one call as a minister is to model grace, not strength. By the grace of God, we have all been rescued from many errors and mishaps by remaining ever sensitive to the still small voice of the Spirit. But this does not overrule the minister's need for seminary, clerical or academic training and mentorship. Astute education, careful guidance and Biblical protocol are all essential in promoting ministerial growth, development, and proper function while avoiding confusion.

Wisdom, built upon applied Biblical knowledge and informed experience, will help you refine your God-given gifts, especially in this changing age of modernity and technology. This is especially true in the public arena. Because of blinding fast advances in communication, people are more aware of God's Word now than at any point in history. This presents incredible opportunities . . . and dangers.

More than likely, your words and appearance as presenter or officiant at Christian ceremonies and traditions are being recorded or broadcast live. This means that your time in front of a seemingly limited group will potentially exist for years online for all the world to see. This is a powerful opportunity that ministers of ages past could never imagine. You now have the ability to reach the world for Christ in all that you do, bringing the hope of His Salvation to everyone, everywhere.

However, there are pitfalls to this same great dynamic. When you put something, or someone puts something featuring you, on the Internet, it remains there for as long as the Lord allows the web to exist. This is why it is so important to "get it right the first time." There are no "second takes" when you are sharing the Gospel to an attentive gathering of emotion-filled people. Viral videos of "fails" are proof of this reality for today's ministers. What little room for error existed in the life of the Christian leader has been completely and permanently removed. As such, if you are uploading material, even if it is just an email to one person, pray before you press "send" or "share."

That is what makes this handbook so important. Use it as your constant companion in making sure that your personal delivery of Christian faith, hope, and love is made at the highest level of excellence.

Most seminary graduates feel unprepared and under-trained for the tasks facing them upon starting their pastorate. While this handbook will assist you in many of your daily tasks as a minister of the Gospel, it is by no means a complete or exhaustive roadmap through all areas of ministerial practice. This is but one guide of many you will need. No matter how prepared you are in your calling, confusion, mishaps, blunders, conflicts, immorality, rumors, and family troubles will arise. This happens because so much is at stake, not the least of which are the eternal destinies of God's children.

Satan, our great adversary, does not want you to succeed as a minister or leader. He does not want you to walk people out of darkness into God's marvelous light (1 Peter 2:9). Yet, you will succeed because God said, "I will never leave you or forsake you." (Hebrews 13:5)

So, whether you are a minister, deacon, trustee, teacher, small group facilitator, usher, choir member or work in the nursery, we are all God's servants, called to be His hands and feet in equipping the saints to do the work of His ministry. As leaders, we should always:

    Love God
        Love People
            Share Christ
                Make Disciples

Author's Note

As an instructor of ministers for several years, many of my graduating students have asked me to recommend a written source they can take with them while serving in the community. While there are many excellent handbooks from which to choose, I have found some of them either outdated or lacking in certain areas.

Ministers at all levels of experience need help and a reliable source of information and guidance without having to "reinvent the wheel." This handbook is meant to provide that kind of assistance. It will aid you, the leader, in performing worship services, weddings, funerals, baptisms, hospital and home visits, dedications, and administering the Sacraments, etc. *Words of Grace* also provides today's minister and leader with several relevant and provocative topics which are easily accessed through the table of contents. Each topic has time-tested principles accompanying it which will help you approach all aspects of ministry with more confidence.

I understand that each church and denomination have their own spiritual protocol and ministerial code of ethics. Therefore, this handbook will by no means bind you to any given set of criteria. Instead, it provides a benchmark so you can customize your service, ceremony, prayer, or ritual *based on the Gospel* – upon which we all agree.

I have also provided a plethora of additional resource materials such as: examples of service, instructions, liturgies, and guides in order for you to combine what is presented here with what you already know or have been taught. Along with peer support and prayer, this will allow you to create your own ceremony format.

I hear many believers and ministers alike say they wished they knew the perfect will of God for their lives. In practice, the answer is simple. Act like Jesus and you are always in God's perfect will. Look to Him, who simply lived what He preached and taught because it flowed from who He is. Learning is caught, not taught. Ministers and church leaders are required to read the Word, study it, meditate on it and ultimately, live it.

As God's patient ambassadors, we are to provide a gentle manner, easy smile, helpful suggestions, clear explanations, and warm, loving insight to soften the journey of life's challenges for all people.

Easily said, not easily done.

Be shepherds of God's flock that is under your care, serving as overseers-not because you must, but because you are willing, as God wants you to be; not greedy for money, but eager to serve; not lording it over those entrusted to you, but being examples to the flock. And when the Chief Shepherd appears, you will receive the crown of glory that will never fade away.
- 1 Peter 5:2-4

Here are some tough questions to ask yourself as you begin each day. Am I a role model and a Godly example to my congregants? Our calling as leaders is always a process of self-analysis. I want people to be on time. Am I? I want people to be prepared when they come to service. Am I? I want people to treat me with courtesy and respect. Do I treat them this way? I have expectations and goals for my congregation. Do they have any for me? Everything must be integrated into our own behavior first if we want the people we are leading to grow sincerely in these areas.

Remember, just because you are the pastor does not excuse you from practicing what you preach. This sounds so obvious. But all of us have seen too many pastors fall from grace for the most obvious of sins.

Acknowledgements

A great deal of research and many resources have been utilized in the production of this handbook, along with over fifteen years in ministry leadership at my home church, The First Cathedral in Bloomfield, Connecticut. With it, I have attempted to produce the type of a handbook that I needed while performing the ministerial duties of my calling.

I am indebted to Archbishop LeRoy Bailey, Jr., Pastor Glenn Davis, Pastor David Fothergill, the late Dr. Horace Holloman, Dr. Ernestine Roberts, Rev. Fred Lawrence, Pastor Eugene Young, and Elder Calvin Hudson, as well as many other colleagues who have poured into my life making this project possible.

Thank you Dr. Justin Irving, Dr. Sam Rima, Dr. Steve Sandage, Dr. Mark McCluskey, Dr. Frank Green and Dr. Greg Bourgond for your support and guidance through my doctoral degree and seminary education at Bethel Seminary in St. Paul, MN.

Thank you Raymond Bechard for your gifts and keen eye in the editing.

Many thanks to Cindie Cagenello for aiding in the layout and design.

This handbook is offered with prayer and great humility to my fellow leaders in the Lord Jesus Christ and I hope they find it helpful while serving in the vineyard.

Rev. Dr. Michael Morawski

The Lordship of Christ

The Other Ships

"And the same day, when the evening was come, he saith unto them, let us pass over unto the other side. And when they had sent away the multitude, they took him even as he was in the ship. And there were also with him other little ships."
—Mark 4:35-36 KJV

"The greatest judgment against man on earth is that God will let him have his way."
—Warren Wiersbe

This handbook is meant to make you a better leader. As such, we begin with your relationship to the fundamental, basic truth of Christianity. We do this because all of us have witnessed leaders who tragically approach their position only as a means of employment. There are far too many for whom being a leader is just a job.

The horrible truth is that there are Christian leaders who are not yet saved.

Think of the implications of this. If they have not received Jesus Christ as their Lord and Savior, how are they, as a leader, going to convince someone else to receive Him? *If the part of the dough offered as firstfruits is holy, then the whole batch is holy; if the root is holy, so are the branches.* - Romans 11:16

If someone has a calling to become a minister,

they must eventually realize there is a divine Caller. You must know, or at least be open to the possibility, that Christ who created you and called you is the only one who knows who you can be. Our life's purpose, therefore, comes from one source, but two directions: who we are *created* to be and who we are *called* to be.

Not only is this Call of our Creator the source of the deepest self-discoveries and growth in life, but it also gives us the inspiration and power that transforms our lives into a creation beyond any comparison.[1]

Let us be clear: your God-placed role in Christian ministry is also your God-placed role in His Kingdom. You have been called to care for the eternal souls of His children. Everything you do echoes forever. This awesome responsibility is never to be taken lightly. Therefore, let us continue seeking ways to improve our personal ministry as we draw ever closer to our Lord.

As a minister of Jesus Christ, you must fully understand the *Lordship of Christ*. Without this, most of what you say and do in His service will not make sense nor will it have a positive impact. Imagine a boat, large or small, pushing its way through the water. By the action of its forward movement, it leaves a clear path, a wake, behind itself. The center of this wake is a channel of smooth water, making it much easier and safer for other boats going in the same direction. Rather than navigate in the rough seas of open water, following the path of the lead ship is the best way to make the journey.

So it is with the leader's calling. You must align yourself with the *Lordship of Christ*, following in the path set forth by Him. The Lordship of Christ is the lead ship of your life.

Every Christian leader must settle the Lordship question in their personal life and calling before they are capable of producing eternal fruit for the Kingdom. If you are saved, Jesus Christ is your Savior. But have you given Him His rightful position as Lord over your life? Have you given Him His rightful position as your doctor? Is He your lawyer? Is He your banker? Is He your counselor?

Jesus is the great I Am! *Then the word of the Lord came to Jeremiah, "I am the Lord, the God of all mankind, is anything too hard for me?"* - Jeremiah 32:26-27

Righteousness must always supersede ritual. Christ Himself is the Supreme Being. He dwells in unapproachable light and is the Creator and the Lord of all things. *He is the image of the invisible God, the firstborn over all creation. For by him all things were created, things in heaven and on earth, visible and invisible, whether thrones or powers or rulers or authorities, all things were created by him and for him.* - Colossians 1:15-16

It is a question of reliance. Who do you rely on to gain wisdom pertaining to the pressing issues in your life and calling? Are you relying on your friends, your traditions, the internet . . . or on your Lord and Savior, Jesus Christ?

All ministers, their congregations, and every person on this earth is in a constant state of *becoming*. When you arrive, God is already there waiting for you. His Word and Truth are forever a part of you, infused into your soul. The Bible provides the perfect approach to this dynamic. It does not attempt to prove the existence of God nor Christ as Creator, it simply accepts it.

The same is true for the approach you take for your life and ministry. How others see the Lord Jesus is determined by how they perceive His ambassadors on earth, the men and women of God. Never forget that you may be the only true representative of Jesus people will ever meet. The only Word of God they hear may be from your lips and life.

This means putting the Lord Jesus first, before all things. It means removing yourself from the throne of your life and placing Christ there permanently, back where He belongs. When you do this, you will experience a life-altering, eternal shift toward holiness.

The Lord said to Moses, "Speak to the entire assembly of Israel and say to them: Be holy because I, the Lord your God, am holy." - Leviticus 19:1-2

Some of your other **ships** that must be aligned with the Lordship of Jesus Christ are:

1. **Wor*ship*** – As a leader for the Lord Jesus Christ, you will never stop worshipping God. This calls for complete and utter reverence for God, deep respect for His holiness, supreme honor for who He is, and the submission of all you are to God.
2. **Leader*ship*** – God Himself is the One who has called you to minister to His flock. He is your Compass, your Direction, and your Destination. However, this does not mean leading your flock on this eternal journey will be easy. As a leader, you are in for the battle of your life. There will be days of grace, loss, fortune, hardship, and victory. Sometimes being the leader gives you the best seat

and the worst seat in the house.[2]

3. **Disciple*ship*** – As a leader, you have important duties and responsibilities that must be carried out in order to reproduce yourself as a disciple. This means that your righteousness comes before your rituals. Your love of Jesus as His disciple is your motivation. Without this dynamic, you are not a leader - *you are an actor.*

4. **Mentor*ship*** – The future is going to need your Godly legacy. This is why you must inspire and guide those coming up behind you. Remember Elijah had only one disciple, Elisha — and look what he did!

5. **Steward*ship*** – You have been blessed so that you may bless others. Learn and put into practice the proper utilization and management of all the resources God has provided you. This is one of the strongest ways to demonstrate His glory and bring about the betterment of His creation.[3] Yet, so many are undone by exploiting their gifts.

6. **Member*ship*** – As a child of God, you have rights in the fellowship of His Kingdom. This is your inherent member*ship*. You belong on this journey with Jesus. Yet, as Christian leaders, we have given up our rights to all complaining, selfishness, self-centeredness, bitterness, boasting, and vanities. The ego is thrown overboard. The church is an *organism*, not an organization. It is the living, physical and spiritual body of Christ on earth. When all the members - God's children - act in unity, exercising their various gifts and functions, Christ is honored through the largest family of

loving people in the world.
7. **Fellow*ship*** – You are not alone. There will be many times when you feel isolated, lonely, disenfranchised, even abandoned. But this is a lie told by the enemy. The truth is that you share an eternal, intimate bond of common friend*ship*, purpose, and devotion that binds Christians together and to Christ. This is why it is so essential that you continue to know and better your relation*ship* with your shipmates. All believers participate together in the saving power and message of the Gospel. Think of a ship with no rivets or welds to hold it together. It disintegrates and sinks. Fellowship is one of the most essential bonds for building unity in the life of the church (Philippians 2:1-4).

Names of God

The Bible refers to our Lord by many names. Here is a convenient way to know and understand the various Names of God.

Name of God	Meaning	Reference
Elohim	God	Genesis 1:1
Yahweh	The Lord	Exodus 6:2-3
El Elyon	God Most High	Psalms 7:17
El Shaddai	God Almighty	Psalms 91:1
Jehovah Yireh	The Lord My Provider	Genesis 22:13-14
Jehovah Nissi	The Lord My Banner	Exodus 17:15
Adonai	Lord	Deuteronomy 6:4
Jehovah Shalom	The Lord is Peace	Judges 6:24
Jehovah Sabaoth	The Lord of Hosts	Isaiah 6:1-3
Jehovah Tsidkenu	The Lord is Our Righteousness	Jeremiah 23:6

The Call

The Call is your personal invitation, summons, or commission from God to form a ministry or to be part of an existing ministry. Never forget that this is *God's initiative*. His Call on your life means totally giving all that you are and all that you do to God and His purposes. The title of "Minister" is nothing more than a fancy way of saying *servant*.

Ministry *is* service.

This means that our primary goal as ministers/servants of God is to administer His grace to others as Christ does for us.

Grace is God's unmerited favor toward mankind. Think of G.R.A.C.E. this way: **G**od's **R**iches **At C**hrist's **E**xpense. Answering God's Call on your life means devoting yourself to dispensing His grace through absolutely everything you do and say... and everything you *don't do* and *don't say*.

The monumental realization that God has personally summoned you for ministry creates a dynamic turning point in your life. He is asking you to respond by investing everything you are, everything you do, and everything you have with utter devotion to His service.[4]

Consequently, you must have full confidence in the fact that God has called you to succeed in His Service. He does not anoint anyone to fail in the ministry. God never plans for some leaders to fail and others to succeed. Those who fail were most likely never called or they were hopelessly unfaithful. You cannot live out your calling with a mere halfhearted effort. You must fully apply yourself to the work God has called you do. Dedicate all of you to all of Him.

Your Call is like the many stages of life. It is always evolving. Usually, new leaders start out in one area of ministry and then migrate to another specialty or level according to the leading of the Holy Spirit. For instance, Paul did not start out as an apostle, and Philip started out in the ministry of helps before he became an evangelist.

It can be foolish to despise the small things. - Zechariah 4:10

As a minister or Christian leader, do not try to be right all the time. There is no merit in always being right. True merit is found only in your character.

When you have a divine Call on your life, you will have conviction and a compulsion in your soul. As you prove faithful to what God gives you, He will trust you with more, all the while He is maturing you spiritually.

There are also very good reasons *not* to enter the ministry:
1. You think it is a good idea or glamorous.
2. Someone else said you should.
3. You saw a need.

The Call to ministry will be confirmed by a call experience. As Moses had his burning bush and Paul was knocked off his high horse, each person will have a select Call by God to be His chosen minister. Your Call into ministry does not have to be this dramatic, but you will have an experience. Was it a dream, vision or prophecy over your life? When you trace your Call, did you find it went all the way back to childhood?

You might be unsure of how your Call was or will be played out, yet you *must be sure* that God has called you. Before you pursue the Call of God on your life, you must understand it is to be taken very seriously. You may be able to fool your seminary professor, senior pastor, Bishop, priest, or whoever, but you cannot fool the living God. Scripture says it is a dreadful thing to fall into the hands of the living God (Hebrews 10:31). Above all, remember that you were chosen as a leader by God Himself and you have been given the greatest privilege and responsibility in all the world. You are to be a pattern of the glorious truth that God saves sinners, a living example of God's mercy and grace in the flesh.

The principles of Christians or "little Christs" or "called ones" takes on great significance in the New Testament:

- There is the goal of the calling. We are called to salvation, holiness and faith (2 Thessalonians 2:13-15).
- Called to the Kingdom and Glory of God (1 Thessalonians 2:12).
- Called to an eternal inheritance (Hebrews 9:15).
- Called to fellowship (1 Corinthians 1:9).
- Called to service (Galatians 1).
- The means of calling is through grace (Ephesians 2:8-9) and through the hearing of the Gospel (2 Thessalonians 2:14).
- The starting point for the divine Call is not works, but the purpose and grace of God in Christ Jesus.

- ❑ The nature of God's calling is described as an upward (Philippians 3:14), heavenly (Hebrews 3:1), holy (2 Timothy 1:9) calling.
- ❑ Christians are urged to lead lives that are worthy of their calling (Ephesians 4:1) and to make their calling and election sure (2 Peter 1:10).[5]

Here are some guidelines to understand the seriousness of your Call to Christ and His ministry for your life:

1. **Know His Voice** - We each hear three voices inside of our conscience all day long. It is either God, the devil or your own soul. The latter provides motivation from your mind, self-will and emotions. It is essential to your ministry that you learn the Master's voice (Matthew 10:19-20). This calls for discernment of all your thoughts and actions.
2. **Give Total Commitment** - Now is the time to give all of yourself to the Kingdom through ministry. This requires Holy Spirit energy. Like an airplane trying to take off from the runway, you must do ministry full throttle.
3. **Humble Yourself** - Humility is a protective shield. Sin cannot exist in the same place as God. If you possess known ongoing sin, it is not from God and you cannot enter His presence. Denying your *self* is the first step in ridding yourself of sin. Humble yourself and claim the protection of God (Psalm 91).
4. **Credibility** - Everything you say as a minister or lay leader must be based on the Bible. Moreover,

everything you *do* in your position must be rooted in the Bible. It is imperative that you *"live the Word."*

5. **Prioritization** - Put your life in proper order. Your relationship to God must be first, then your family, then your ministry.

6. **Deliverance** - Whether you know it or not, you may be under the influence of ancient sin. Do not dismiss this very real possibility. Break any known and unknown generational curses in your family line (Nehemiah. 9:2, Daniel. 9:8). Without freeing yourself from this entrapment, you may never be capable of escaping the devil's grasp.

7. **Prove Yourself Faithful** - Seeing your ministry come to its fulfillment will take time and patience. And these take continual faith. At first, your Call will be scattered. Then it will take on significance, order and meaning.

8. **Vigilance** - God will use many different channels to communicate with you. You must be forever on the lookout for His genuine directives for you. He will talk to you directly in your spirit, through His Word, through prayers, dreams, visions, songs, movies, books, signs, and through other people.

9. **Belief** - God's timing is perfect. Shed all doubt and know you are called to be a leader for such a time as this.

10. **Obedience** - Learn not only to hear from God, but to intensely *obey* Him. As a leader, remind yourself each morning that you must hear and obey the Master (John 16:12).

11. **Truth** - Truth is not a thing, it is a *Person* (John 14:6). Speak only that Truth, the Truth that God gives you

through Jesus. This is the only way to build a circle of trust from the Lord through you to the people of your ministry. God will not trust His Word to believers who do not keep theirs.

12. **Punctuality** - Arrive early for your commitments. Be eager to begin. As a leader, if you arrive right on time, you are late.
13. **Financial Integrity** - This is one of the most important elements of the ministry. Learn the power of the finances God has allotted to you and how to handle them properly. Any amount of money comes with responsibility. You are responsible for your money and your ministry's money.
14. **Sexual Purity** - This is the most dangerous element in the ministry. As an ambassador for Christ, your life must always be one of complete reverence for God. Wise leaders will keep themselves accountable to others in this area.
15. **Character** - Do not compromise the principles of God to gain the blessings of God . . . or the empty praise of people. God will not honor this behavior. Carry yourself in a way that honors God and God will honor your ministry.

Entering any calling in life is a serious matter that merits prayerful consideration, a searching of God's Word, and keen observation of providential leadings.[6] This is particularly true of your Call to ministry. The Bible describes the role of leaders and labels them accordingly: overseer, guardian, ruler, feeder, prayer warrior, watchman, teacher of sound doctrine, example to believers, leader, sacrificial servant, wise counselor, bearer of burdens, keeper of unity, protector of the flock, and worshipper to name a few.[7] The Apostle Paul describes some attributes and qualities the leader must possess after realizing their internal Call by God. These are found in 1 Timothy 3 and Titus 1.

Martyn Lloyd Jones, Pastor of London's Westminster Chapel, prolific author and regarded by many as the greatest 20th-century reformed preacher, affirms the ministerial Call with the following generalities:

1. A Call generally starts in the form of a consciousness within one's own spirit.
2. The Call is accentuated through the influence of others.
3. The Call develops and leads to a concern for others.
4. Those called should possess a sense of constraint.
5. Those called will have a sense of humility signified by diffidence, unworthiness, and inadequacy.
6. Anyone called must be sent by the church.

Dr. Lloyd-Jones states that the church must look for the following qualifications in those who will serve in its ministry. A person who:

1. Is filled with the Spirit.
2. Has knowledge of the Truth and their relationship to it.
3. Has good character, Godliness, wisdom, patience, gentleness, etc.
4. Has understanding of people and of human nature.
5. Has natural intelligence and ability.

6. Has the gift of speech.[8]

In summary, we may conclude that the ministerial calling is a *holy calling* which involves the following:

1. Holy Life
This is a prerequisite to the Call itself. A holy life must flow out of a genuine conversion (acceptance of Jesus Christ as Lord and Savior). There must be attributes of Godliness manifest in the called person's life, such as are found in 1 Timothy 3 and Titus 1. Those called by God must also be exercising the principles of Godliness in their family relationships, their sexual morality, their finances, and in all areas of their life. (It is not enough to avoid the "Danger Zones," the leader must revel in the "Holy Zone.")

2. Holy Desire
This is your wholehearted desire to do the work of the ministry, by the Holy Spirit, through Scripture and providence. Some of God's servants are called through the application of specific texts or scriptural passages. Others are called through intervening acts of providence, directing and burdening them with an intense commitment toward and desire for the ministry. No matter what form it takes, one's Call must conform to Scripture and be strengthened by the timing and circumstances of providence. All of this compels the minister to give oneself to the work of the ministry.

3. Holy Motivation

The Call must be motivated by a love for the glory of God and the proclamation of the Gospel of Christ Jesus. These, combined with the burden of love for souls, and the needs of the church create an unstoppable motivation in the heart of the minister.

4. Holy Compulsion

There must be a growing sense of Spirit-filled compulsion for this work. Your soul must be crying out, "Woe unto me if I preach not the Gospel." This compulsion will involve a sense of self-denial and the earnest desire to live wholeheartedly for God.

5. Holy Fitness

There must be some measure of ministerial and speaking gifts, some aptitude in teaching, some spiritual maturity (in the experience of one's own misery, deliverance, and gratitude), some knowledge of Scripture, some wisdom of doctrinal and spiritual matters, some gift of prayer, some awareness of human nature and an understanding of and compassion for people.

6. Holy Struggles

Your ministerial Call will not come to fruition without strife and continual self-examination. Intense struggles concerning the ministerial Call are commonplace. These include struggles with:

a. Surrendering to the work
b. The weight of the work
c. Satan's devices aimed to thwart the Call
d. One's unworthiness for and inability to do that work
e. The need for confirmation of the Call itself

7. Holy Confirmation

The inward Call is confirmed commonly by the approbation of God's people, and must always be confirmed by a congregation's actual Call to the person who has completed their seminary training. The Call of the church is also part of the person's Call to the ministry. Thus, the Call is a gradual process which does not culminate until one's ordination; in fact, this Call is in process of being fulfilled throughout the entire life of the minister.

8. Holy Spirit

Though this list may be helpful in contemplating and evaluating a ministerial Call, the Call itself cannot be reduced to a mere menu of items. Ultimately, the Call is the work of the Holy Spirit in each one of the points explained above. The minister alone must and will fulfill the ministerial Call that God plants and nourishes in His own time and way.[9]

If your Call has been confirmed, the minister's work has just begun. God is a God of order and each duty performed by the minister must be done in the spirit of excellence. Whether conducting some impressive rite of the church, or preaching the Word, or ministering to the poor, or helping with some menial tasks around the house, every opportunity has, at all times, the possibility of making honorable the high calling of God.[10]

Ministerial Ethics and Spiritual Protocol

Principles of Conduct

By common consent, the Christian ministry is to be esteemed more than any other profession. People see Christian ministers as spokespersons for God Himself and they expect the behavior of ministers to be exceedingly moral and just, more so than anyone else in society. Ministers are not to take their high calling as a mark of personal honor to themselves, but as an honor to the One who first called them.

From the acknowledged truth that the ministry is the highest form of professional service, come foundational principles upon which any consideration of the minister's conduct must be based. **As such, the leader must:**

1. Keep the nobility of the calling uppermost in their mind.
2. Take the high moral ground in all their actions in order to lift the reputation of the Christian ministry.
3. Never forget that they are the one who serves God and others. Therefore, be on guard against any and all temptations the profession presents.
4. Never, for reasons of personal safety, desert the church and people when any danger looms or attacks, such as a hostile invasion, epidemic, natural disaster, or terrorist attack.
5. Utilize time properly.

6. Resist measuring the vocation by the salary involved, or the grading of other ministers by the size of their respective salaries. This degrades the whole profession.
7. Guard the use of their name. The leader should not give sanction or endorsement to questionable causes or movements.
8. Not encroach upon the field of another profession. They must know when they have reached the limit of their abilities and gifts. There is great wisdom in calling upon the expertise of others, such as counseling, financial advice, and medical treatment.
9. Not debase the profession by becoming a handyman for all the members of the church. Be careful about lending money, automobiles, purchasing tickets, and generally running errands for the community. Don't be a jack of all trades. Be a master of one, for the One who is the Master.
10. Hold their professional service in such esteem that it rises above the distractions and confusion so commonplace in today's ministry. Before the Christian minister can *do* anything, they must first *be* something.[11]

Practical Protocol for Associate Ministers, Assistant Pastors and Lay Leaders

As one who serves those who serve, conduct yourself in a way that continually adds spiritual and professional value to your senior pastor or senior leader. This should be the heart cry of every associate minister: to be profitable to the person of God for whom they work. The following principles by A.R. Williams will help make you even more profitable to your leader:

1. **Serve, As Serving Unto The Lord.** (Ephesians 6:5-8). Even though you are assisting another by working under their umbrella of ministry, you must realize that you are ultimately working for the Lord. Your commitment to the Lord must transcend your commitment to the leader over you. Give 100%.
2. **Learn All You Can About The Pastor And The Church.** (1 Thessalonians 5:12-13). Study the pastor. Watch, listen, observe, and absorb. The better you know your leader, the better you will be able to adapt yourself and be a blessing to the ministry.
3. **Be Willing To Earn The Pastor's Trust**. (Philippians 2:19-21). Do not demand certain levels of authority or responsibility, earn them. Do not be bothered if the pastor does not want you to do certain things. If you establish a solid, and trusting

relationship with the pastor, then you will gradually be given increased responsibility.

4. **Be Correctable.** (Proverbs 15:10). Do not insist on doing everything your own way. As the associate, let the pastor know you want their help and advice throughout your ministry. Act on what you are instructed to do and your ministry will be a blessing.

5. **Be Accountable To The Pastor.** (Acts 20:28, Hebrews 13:17). Accountability is scriptural. It helps keep the pastor in touch with your ministry and the lives within the flock. It also motivates your goal setting and will enhance your effectiveness.

6. **Understand The Proper Flow Of Authority.** (1 Peter 2:18-23). Work with the church from where they are, not from where you are. Focus on your ministry and do not interfere with other areas of authority.

7. **Connect Yourself To The Pastor's Vision.** When there are two visions in a church, you have a di-vision. Execute the pastor's vision with the same dedication and enthusiasm you would give your own. Go about your ministry as your ultimate calling and the most important thing you will ever do. Do not use your pastor's ministry as a platform to build your own ministry.

8. **Keep Your Pulpit Ministry Compatible To The Pastor.** Keep your messages basic and do not try to outperform your senior pastor. Your viewpoint should always be publicly in line with the leaders above you.

9. **Release the Pastor From Some Responsibilities.** (Acts 6:1-6). Pastors are terribly burdened. This is why they love to hear the words, "Is there anything more I can do for you?" Make yourself available to hold your pastor up at all times and in all ways.
10. **Encourage Your Pastor.** (Proverbs 25:13, Philippians 2:3-4). Express personal appreciation when he or she has been a blessing to you. Pass on good reports from the congregation. Pastors hear many negative reports, it is refreshing to hear the good.
11. **Publicly Support Your Pastor.** Always present the pastor in a positive light. The unity of God's people creates an effective ministry to others. Be to your pastor what you would want your associates to be to you.
12. **Be An Asset, Not A Liability.** Never make trouble - *ever* - and do not be the source of problems. Not everyone in the church is a fan of the pastor, but the associate minister must be. As an associate, you are the solution for whom your pastor has been praying.
13. **Know What To Do With What You Have Learned.** As you study, be sure you do not think that you know more about the church than your pastor. Remember, God has placed you both in your respective positions for His reasons. Respect that Authority and apply what you have learned for the benefit of your given tasks. When you feel you know what is better for the church than anyone else, it might be time to go.
14. **Be Tolerant With The People Of The Church.** (Galatians 5:22). There were problems before you

arrived and they will be there after you have gone. Your job is to exhibit the compassion and grace of Jesus. Do not try to fix everyone, everything, or every problem. Letting frustration overtake you will drastically reduce your effectiveness as an associate.

15. **Do Not Buck The System.** (1 Samuel 19:29). This does not mean the system does not need change or that you cannot play some role in changing it. It all depends on your approach, which should be kind and patient. Wisdom will teach you to adapt yourself to the pastor and the church. Do not try to change too much, too quickly. God did not send you there to change everything to your liking. You are there to serve the pastor and the people.

16. **Do Not Be An Absalom.** (2 Samuel 15, Jeremiah 23:1-4). We read in the Bible that Absalom stole the hearts of the people. In the spiritual realm, one who leads a rebellion has already proven they have a critical nature, no matter how angelic their ways are. This is the sign of an unprincipled character and hidden motives in their heart. This person creates dissatisfaction and tension by seizing power or siphoning followers away from the ministry. Ultimately, God will not bless a foundation of followers built on insurrection.

17. **Do Not Take Over The Pastor's Job.** It could be that an associate minister will someday replace the pastor, but the associate should never do anything to hasten that transition. If God has revealed this to you, let Him bring it to pass in His good time.

18. **Leave Right.** If you remain faithful to your pastor

and apply the aforementioned principles, God will honor and exalt you by establishing you in your own ministry (Luke 16:12). When you get the green light from God, leave with love, respect and the blessing of your pastor and the people. You cannot afford to leave in strife.

Author Mark Barclay in his book, *Beware of Seducing Spirits* states, "The most deadly snare and weapon that Satan uses against associate ministers and assistant pastors is to get them involved in criticism, fault-finding and listening to negative church members."

Guidelines for Detecting Negative Spirits

✝

It might be time to check yourself as an associate minister, assistant pastor or leader when you find yourself exhibiting a rebellious Absalom spirit by the following:

- ❏ You judge other church members.
- ❏ You begin to wish you were in charge.
- ❏ You think and say, "If only I were pastor…"
- ❏ You are convinced that your pastor is too busy for you and does not care.
- ❏ You feel comfortable running with those who have been placed under church discipline or who are known troublemakers.
- ❏ You begin to associate with people who share the same problems you have.
- ❏ You become ensnared in church politics while kissing cheeks and putting down your pastor.
- ❏ You accuse the pastor of being too hard, strict and untouchable.
- ❏ You finally march against your own church leadership, but only to your own failure.

These are only the first red flags in your spirit as a leader. If you are not careful, you might also be suffering from the spirit of Korah (Numbers 16), which is a spirit of discontentment. **Here are some warning signs:**

- ❏ You are critical of your pastor's style.
- ❏ You want to be in leadership in order to expedite

your priorities in your way.
- ❏ You watch and judge the pastor rather than obey the Word and help the people.
- ❏ You begin to openly and publicly challenge your pastor.
- ❏ You band together in little private meetings and/or start impeachment.
- ❏ You think the anointing has left you and yell, "Cult!" "Unfair!" "It's not of God!" etc.
- ❏ You ultimately leave the church because your scheme failed and your pride drives you out.

The Six C's

Today's leaders would do well to consider building their lives on the framework of six principles: Character. Competence. Chemistry. Connectivity. Commitment. Courage. Once Christ has been established as the solid Rock of the leader's foundation, the building process upon The Six C's has commenced. One can be a great preacher, teacher and counselor, excel at weddings, baptisms, funerals, dedications, be ordained, hold the title of Senior Pastor or Bishop, but this is only what the people know of the public persona. The work is tested by the true character of the inner self.

Character – God might elevate you to a position, but your character will keep you there. Of The Six C's, your character is the most obvious to all, and the one most often equated with trust. Yet, character is hardest to assess. Character can be defined as a leader's sense of moral fortitude, an inner compass that determines how a person acts when no one else is looking. Other definitions use terms like reputation, integrity, virtue, and core ethical values.

At its root, Godly character reflects the idea of *etching*, something that is so deep, it not only identifies a person, but also defines them. Remember, God truly is the only One who defines who you are as a person, not anyone or anything else. This is why it is so important to demonstrate the good qualities the Lord has placed in you; people will judge God by what they see in your character.

Ministry leaders would agree in principle that character is important. Yet in reality, many leaders and organizational systems allow competence and communication to stand in for character. While doing so may result in short-term success, eventually the faults in an individual's true character surface. The revelation will not only erase much of their success, it can potentially ruin that leader's reputation for a lifetime. Time will tell, of course. Time will *always* tell. That's the nature of character: it is proven over time, in multiple settings, both in the public eye and outside of it.[12]

The Scriptures discuss character as something that has been proven and approved. The Apostle Paul said in 2 Corinthians 5:10, *"We must all appear before the judgment seat of Christ, that each one may receive what is due him for the things done while in the body, whether good or bad."* The message here is very clear: *be very careful how you live.*

Competence – Competence is simply the ability to do something well, the quality or state of being competent. Paul said, *"For we are God's workmanship, created in Christ Jesus to do good works, which God prepared in advance for us to do."* – Ephesians 2:10. What does this mean for the minister of the 21st century? Quite simply, if you claim to have a calling to become a preacher, you should be able to preach. If you claim to be a teaching minister, you should be able to teach, anytime, anywhere and with any material.

God has determined this calling for you. He prepared you to do it. To enhance your gifts, you must have an extensive, ongoing capacity to build your core competence. This means having a working library including several Bible versions, commentaries, lexicons, Bible encyclopedias, dictionaries, and devotional classics, as well as several books on prayer and the promises of God.

Primary to the calling and work is a minister's personal duty to cultivate his or her own spiritual life. You cannot lead anyone where you have not traveled. Be very careful as a minister that your familiarity with sacred things does not breed pride. The Bible becomes a quarry out of which to dig texts, not a reservoir for personal spiritual refreshment. Prayer is something mostly done for others.[13]

Our contact with the holy is not merely an encounter with a different dimension of reality; it is a meeting with Absolute Reality. Christianity is not about involvement with religious experience as a tangent. It involves meeting with a holy God, who forms the center, or core, of human existence. The Christian faith is theocentric. God is not at the edge of Christians lives, but at the very center. God defines our entire life and worldview.[14]

This is how the Christian minister takes hold of competence, by letting God take hold of the minister.

Nothing teaches like experience. A minister must constantly hone their craft. Volunteer to assist with weddings, baptisms, funerals and anything else you can do to increase your skill levels.

Chemistry – To know Christ and to make Him known requires a Christian minister or leader to interact with others, sometimes under adverse circumstances. You need to remember, the person is as much the message as are their words.[15] It has been said that your personality and disposition are formed before you reach the age of six. God knew exactly the parents you should have to develop your unique personality. But this can be enhanced by hard work and lifelong study. When you truly understand God's love for you, then you will be compelled to love others.

A minister or Christian leader should develop chemistry with others through their passion. Passion is attractive, and a passion for Jesus is irresistible. We are drawn to people who have passion for the divine in their lives because it indicates we are talking to a person of depth. Never let the ministry you perform become routine. Never let your holy fire go out! We are drawn to passion in others because it kindles our own emotions. Passionate people have a certainty about them, so it is easy to get caught up in their emotional rhythm.

Simply being a nice minister does not develop lasting chemistry. Being "nice" will create an unfulfilled and less satisfying life. Always trying to please others develops a distant coldness leading to a loss of affection. The end result is a possible spirit of resentment.

In building connections with people, remember the words of Zig Ziglar, the Christian motivational speaker, "If you treat everyone as though they are hurting, you will be treating the majority of people in the proper manner." [16]

Connectivity – John Maxwell said, "Everyone communicates, few connect." People need to know you are on their side. How? You need to connect with their feelings, desires, wishes, fears and passions. They need to know they can trust you. People need to know that you understand them and are focused on them. They need to know you find them uniquely interesting and important.

Good connectors understand that people do things for their own reasons, not yours. Consider this question: are you inspired by people who care only about themselves? Self-centered people hardly connect with anyone. **Learn to connect by asking yourself three questions:**

1. *What is this person thinking about the most?* Ask them about their culture, values, responsibilities, and their dreams. When you know what a person thinks about, it helps you to speak their inspirational language. Connectors listen before they share what they think.

2. *What is this person truly saying?* Good connectors are good listeners. They look for the subtext beneath the words they hear. Listen, learn and then lead. When we mix love with honesty, we will tell the right truth to the right person at the right time in the right way for the right reason and we will get a right result.

3. *What is this person doing?* Watch the activities in which they are engaged. Watch their body language, discern their attitudes and observe their energy levels. People need encouragement. It is the little things that yield big results.[17]

Commitment – You might be the greatest minister any seminary has ever produced, tops in your class, totally credentialed, completely cordial and filled with godly character, gifted, anointed, and appointed. Everyone loves you and they cannot wait until you walk into the room – but there is one small problem…you never showed up! You will not be able to bring glory to God, lead anyone to salvation, or perform a single duty for the Body of Christ unless you are committed. Commitment is the state or quality of being devoted to a cause or activity, an obligation that restricts freedom of action and sharply focuses all efforts.

Some people cannot commit, and some will simply not commit. What a person *can* do and what they *will* do are two very different things. Do you suffer from commitment phobia? **Below are some points that may help identify the cause, especially if you have experienced:**

- Trust issues because of past hurts by those close to the person
- Childhood trauma or abuse
- Unmet childhood needs or attachment issues
- Complicated family dynamics while growing up[18]

You must be delivered or set free from these issues if you expect to minister effectively in the present. Do not allow your wounds to control you, turning you into someone you were not meant to be. Follow your dreams, know your talents and passions, believe in yourself, always give your best, heal your wounds, and take the path your spirit is telling you. God will meet you there.

None of these attributes will be nurtured, obtained, or become a part of your life as a Christian leader without the final C of The Six C's - Courage.

Courage – Our fear will always get the better of us. Jesus knew this. Perhaps that is why He told His followers to "fear not" so often. The enemy would like nothing better than for you to be frozen in your fear. You accomplish no good thing for God when terror resides in you. Those who live in fear lead and preach with fear. Like a disease or sin, fear spreads.

Without courage nothing moves. Courage is not being fearless, it is moving forward in spite of fear. In the ministry you will come across many frightening circumstances, but you must proceed. Has your fear made you say or do things that was not coming from you or your passion for Jesus?

Brennan Manning, in his book *ALL IS GRACE*, calls it the "impostor." The impostor is a fake version of who you are. Brennan says his impostor was born when he was eight years old. He faked being happy when he was sad, faked being excited when he was disappointed, and faked being nice when he was very angry inside. He looked and sounded himself, but it honestly was not him. Brennan says bluntly, "I was a fake ... I lived as an impostor of myself." Living as the impostor will do nothing but dehumanize you and make dysfunctional all your relationships (with God, yourself, all others, and the earth). **Here are some characteristics of the impostor, any one of which can just about kill a person:**

- ❏ The impostor lives in fear (the primary motivator in our lives is fear and is the basis for all of these points).
- ❏ The impostor is consumed with a need for acceptance and approval.
- ❏ The impostor is codependent and out of touch with his or her feelings.
- ❏ The impostor's life is herky-jerky existence of elation and depression.
- ❏ The impostor is what he or she does.

- ❏ The impostor demands to be noticed.
- ❏ The impostor cannot experience intimacy in any relationship.
- ❏ And last but not least, the impostor is a liar.[19]

As leaders, to walk by faith and not by sight takes considerable courage. Our courageous freedom to be vulnerable and transparent transforms the way we live, love, parent and lead.[20]

"We don't see things as they are; we see things as we are." – *Anais Nin* [21]

Here is a powerful statement that will assist you in building your courage. Speaking this aloud daily, or as often as possible, transforms your sense of courage: "When I face my fears, I will begin to control my fear." Self-leadership means that I must know myself and have a firm grasp on my strengths as well as my weaknesses. I will not lose myself in my strengths or my weaknesses. I have balance and courage in my personal and professional life. I want to be a better person, but I must discipline myself to acquire the necessary resources to reach the next level. And to go to the next level, I must put away my *self* and my *fears* so that I can be truly courageous.

If you fail to deal with your own issues as a leader, your fears will set your agenda, rather than the Lord and the needs of His people.

Worship Services

Words of Grace now transitions from theology to application offering fresh and timely approaches to sensitive material. Remember, it is not enough for the leader to know what to say and do, it must be done well. So, I have included different examples and suggestions to assist you in the vitally important duties of your ministry.

The Fall of Mankind Explained

No one joins the military and does their own thing; they follow a set of rules designed to prolong life. Consequently, all mankind was condemned to die because of the original sin of Adam passed to the entire human race. *Therefore, just as sin entered the world through one man, and in this way death came to all men, because all sinned.* – Romans 5:12. There was no death before Adam. Man fell in the garden because he and she decided to go it themselves. Now, we suffer many consequences because of this one sin which separated us from God.

Whether you are a Christian or not, you have to admit there is something wrong with mankind throughout the world. Because of the Fall, sin resides deep in the heart of all men and women. It is not something on the surface of their lives. Sin lives right down at the very core of their being. Sin is derived from the original root of the human race, and through Adam all sin has originated. Therefore, sin is not only restricted to one's actions, but it is essentially a condition. Sin is a lack of conformity to the moral law of God, either in state, disposition, or act. This is why we need a Savior, a Rescuer, and a Deliverer. [22]

Why Worship?

The concept and reasons behind worship are simple. Everything was created to glorify God, especially mankind. *For by him [Christ] all things were created: things in heaven and on earth, visible and invisible, whether thrones or powers or rulers or authorities; all things were created by him and for him.* – Colossians 1:16. As believers, we worship Jesus Christ, the One who saved us from sin, death and hell (Romans 6:23).

Man is unique, because there is no creature on earth like him, born with a free-will. He is not driven by instincts like the animals, because God breathed into him the breath of *His* life and man became a living soul (Genesis 2:7). Man is body, mind, self-will, emotions, and spirit, all which long to connect with its Creator. But how does a human being connect with the Supreme Being who created them? What is the bridge that will allow us to crossover and commune with God? How are we reconciled back to a holy God as sinful fallen creatures? The answer to these questions is Jesus.

Jesus is the Answer

We worship Jesus, God incarnate, the Creator who made Himself flesh and dwelt among us (John 1:14). There is no one like the Lord Jesus. He is fully God and fully man simultaneously. But He was no ordinary man. He was a divine human born of a virgin with incorruptible blood, to redeem our fallen humanity back to God the Father. God created us, sustains us and redeems us. Why? Because God loves us and wants an eternal relationship with us. Our supernatural state is to be in the presence of God.

God's love bridges the gap of separation between God and mankind. When Jesus Christ died on the cross and rose from the grave, He paid the penalty for all mankind's sins. Because God and sin cannot occupy the same space, our sins have separated us from God and His ultimate plan for our lives. Peace and life fill His wonderful plan for mankind. But no one can know His peace, life, or salvation until they are born again. Jesus said, "I tell you the truth, no one can see the Kingdom of God unless he is born again" (John 3:3). There is no other way into heaven other than to receive Jesus Christ as your Lord and Savior. Think about it. Jesus did not say He knows a way to God; He said, "I am the way and the truth and the life. No one comes to the Father except through me" (John 14:6). The greatest gift of all is that when you receive Jesus as Lord and Savior, you become His child. *Yet to all who received him, to those who believed in his name, he gave the right to become children of God.* - John 1:12

To receive Christ one needs to do four things:
1. ADMIT your spiritual need. "I am a sinner."
2. REPENT and be willing to turn from your sin.
3. BELIEVE that Jesus Christ died for you on the cross.
4. RECEIVE through prayer, Jesus Christ into your heart and life.[23] (Romans 10:13, Revelation 3:20)

Salvation Prayers

Here are some examples of salvation prayers when inviting people to accept Jesus Christ as their Savior. Instruct them to repeat after you:

Salvation Prayer #1
Dear Father, I confess I have gone my own way and I have sinned against you. I believe in your Son Jesus Christ, whom You sent to die for my sins. He was crucified, died, and was buried. On the third day, You raised Him from the dead and He sits at your right hand. I repent of all of my sins and turn my heart towards You, Father. I now invite Jesus to be my Lord and Savior. Heavenly Father, I thank you for eternal life through Your Son Jesus, Amen.

Salvation Prayer #2
Lord Jesus, I need You. Thank You for dying on the cross for my sins. I open the door of my life and receive You as my Savior and Lord. Thank You for forgiving

my sins and giving me eternal life. Take control of the throne of my life. Make me the kind of person You want me to be.[24]

Principles of Worship

†

The main objective behind any worship service is to glorify God. Likewise, the primary objective of the church is to save souls and promote public worship. Man brings glory to God through private and corporate (public) worship. True worship is not being a spectator; we must actively participate. True worship comes from the human spirit directed towards a holy God (John 4:24). This is accomplished by creating an atmosphere where believers can sense the presence of an awesome God while basking in the community, love, and fellowship of other believers.

During worship, either privately or corporately, believers experience vision, comfort, inspiration, guidance, and direction for living the devoted Christian life. This occurs because we intentionally put our entire focus on the Lord. Worship services may vary greatly according to culture, denominational traditions, generational differences, and the movement of the Holy Spirit. Generally, the content remains unchanged. Each individual believer brings his or her own contribution to the corporate worship service. This mandate comes from Scripture. In Hebrews 10:24-25 we read, *"And let us consider how we may spur one another on toward love and good deeds. Let us not give up meeting together as some are in the habit of doing, but let us encourage one another - and all the more as you see the Day approaching."* What day is that? The day when Christ returns for His Church, the bride without spot, wrinkle, or blemish (Ephesians 5:25-27).

Regardless of your choice of music, liturgy, time of day, length of service, or who does what and when, there are some changeless principles regulating the content of the Christian worship service:

1. **Our expressions of worship must always be grounded in Scripture**. Old and New Testament writings serve as our ultimate authority and source for all worship. The Psalms and doxologies from Paul's writings establish our patterns of worship. [25]
2. **True worship is always directed towards Christ and His redemptive work on the cross**. The good news of the Gospel is the proclamation of Christ, His birth, life, death, resurrection, and ascension bring glory and honor to God the Father through the Holy Spirit.
3. **Worship is expressed through words, actions, music, and other art forms such as drama and dance**. Some examples of expressing worship to God are not limited to, but can include: The reading of Scripture, singing of hymns and other contemporary Christian songs, sermons (the proclamation of the Gospel), personal testimonies, the offering of prayers, presentation of offerings, baby dedications, announcements, and the benediction (blessing).
4. **The act of worshipping the Triune God can**

be expressed many ways. Through adoration, thanksgiving, prayer, healing, music of all kinds, confession, petition, intercession, raising of hands, dancing, joyous shouting, and much more.
5. **Worship is a dialogue between God and man.** We are to actively listen *for* the Lord, as well as express petitions *to* the Lord. During worship, God is especially responsive to His children. God does everything decently and in order; therefore our worship experience should be done in the spirit of excellence, decorum, harmony, and relevance.

Worship Service Ideas

The rest of this chapter provides additional ideas to enhance your worship services. Beginning with appearance, parking lot attendants and greeters; then prayer and an explanation of why music is even used. Also, tips on Scripture reading with power, and how to turn your offering into a time of incredible opportunity. Finally, using the benediction to bring peace, along with various orders of service.

Appearance, Parking Attendants & Greeters

Hundreds, perhaps thousands, of people pass by your church each day. What they consistently see on your property builds their perspective of your entire ministry. Your physical structure and the land upon which it sits represent excellent opportunities to invite new people into your congregation.

However, avoiding negative perceptions requires vigilant upkeep and maintenance. Is your grass cut and your landscaping well manicured? Is your signage easy to see and welcoming? Is there even the slightest bit of trash blowing across the area? Is the snow removed quickly and efficiently? Is the paint peeling?

Your campus exists first and foremost to bring honor and glory to God. Keeping this as a priority will ensure that everything is well manicured, spotless and, at this point in our society, smoke-free.

At first glance, it may seem odd to focus on your selection of parking lot attendants. But use great care in your selection. They create the first impression visitors and new congregants have to the people of your church. As such, the attitude and spirit of parking attendants paint a picture of what will happen inside your church, whether it is accurate or not. They are your only chance to make a good first impression. Make sure you assign people who have good cheer and the patience to assist people in doing one of the things in life that no one likes to do: park their car.

The parking attendants should be smiling, friendly, courteous, and informative if questions are asked. Remember, outreach programs are designed to attract unbelievers to your facility. If your church has recovery groups such as AA or NA, attendees may wish to smoke during breaks if they feel anxious. People matter to God, so bend rules before you break hearts.

A word of caution; be wary of designated parking spaces for staff and dignitaries. The Bible says we are not to show favoritism (Romans 2:11) and new people may feel slighted. A designated section for Visitors located close to the church entrance is always a welcoming gesture. Your church may want to entertain the idea of a valet service or shuttle bus from the parking lot if the need arises. Check with local churches who are currently doing this and model their success.

Greeters are an excellent way to show congregants that your church is a church for all people and that you care. Greeters are your first line of contact for new people entering your church. Greeting people as they enter the facility is more than a handshake and a smile. It is an opportunity to express God's love through Christ and help set the tone of the upcoming worship service. A church greeter is one of the simplest, yet most important positions in the church.

The goal of the greeter is to be compassionately hospitable in all ways possible: smile, share a kind word, open a door, offer a handshake, or just lend a helping hand to people as they enter the church. This may be the only person the visitor speaks to during their time at your church. As such, they are representing Jesus to that person. This is a huge and glorious opportunity.

To effectively and consistently welcome people, develop some church greeter guidelines for your team.
Here are some ideas:
1. Show up on time - early is always best.
2. Always be positive.

3. Prepare yourself spiritually.
4. Be friendly to all who enter.
5. Pray for your ministry in advance.
6. Show honor and dignity toward your visitors and guests.
7. Pay attention to what needs your visitors and guests might have.
8. Follow up after the worship service and say goodbye with sincerity, cheer and grace.
9. Prepare yourself physically: good grooming, appropriate clothing, and fresh breath.
10. Look for ministry opportunities to pray with your guests before they leave.

Remember, your goal is simple and direct: Make people feel welcome at your church! [26]

Prayer of Invocation

Church service is about to commence. Quiet music may be playing through your sound system in the lobby and/or sanctuary as worshippers arrive. People pray and gather in fellowship throughout the church. This may also be a good time for church announcements on video screens, unless you prefer to do them in person from the pulpit or lectern during or at the end of service. Some churches begin with a welcome song urging spontaneous hugs or handshakes as a peace offering. Some churches prefer to hit it hard at the opening with three or four praise songs. Regardless of the method chosen, make people feel welcome, noticed, and loved. This may be the only thing they remember about your church.

The prayer of invocation is a brief introductory prayer invoking (summoning) the Spirit of God and inviting people into His Presence. This opening prayer is a divine invocation of His blessings upon the congregation and is not to be taken lightly. The prayer of invocation should be no longer than one minute and is not a time for any minister or church leader to take it upon themselves to preach or teach.

Here are some examples of sample prayers of invocation:

Sample Prayer #1
O' Heavenly Father, Lord Jesus and Holy Spirit, we invoke your Spirit and your Presence to commune with us right now. Open our mouths that we may show forth your praise, enlighten our minds that we may understand your truth, shower us with your grace, that we may receive what you will have us to do, open our hearts and help us to dedicate our lives to your service. Do what only you can do, take over this service, save, sanctify, set free and deliver your people from the hand of the enemy, in Jesus' most mighty and matchless name we pray, Amen.

Sample Prayer #2
Almighty Father, unto whom all hearts are open, all desires known, and from whom no secrets are hid, cleanse the thoughts of our hearts as a congregation and inspire us by the Holy Spirit that we may perfectly

love you, for you alone are worthy. We magnify your holy name, through Jesus Christ our Lord, Amen.[28]

Sample Prayer #3
Almighty and everlasting God in whom we live and move and have our being, grant to us purity of heart and strength of purpose so that we may seek your will and to live without faltering, for the sake of Jesus Christ, your Son, Amen.[29]

Sample Prayer #4
Father God, in the name of Jesus, we love you and we praise you, we offer up to you the highest praise Lord God, we turn our hearts to you for you alone are worthy, you alone are God most High. Father, we ask you right now to look down on your people and lead us and guide us in the paths of righteousness for your namesake, and let your Spirit flow through these seats and hallways and all over this building, cleanse the recesses of our hearts and minds and call us back into your saving grace and Presence. Thank you, Father for always hearing our prayers. Save and sanctify this day and call your children unto yourself for such a time as this. We will be careful to give you all the praise, honor and glory that you so richly deserve, through Jesus Christ our Lord, Amen.

Hymns of Praise

Hymns of praise set to music or Scripture, are songs that may be committed to memory and sung. Hymns may be announced or spontaneously initiated by the leader or worshippers. Both the Scripture songs and the hymns should point worshippers to God, His activity and attributes.[30]

There are many options for music in a church setting. Make sure the music leads the people into an atmosphere of worship, keeping in mind the milieu of your culture. We are not to entertain the congregation, thus making us like the world. We are to worship Almighty God; *we are never to worship our worship.*

Every church is unique and has its own culture. Some churches attract new believers and raise Christians from the beginning of their faith journey. Other churches specialize in reaching certain ethnicities or languages, while others focus on life issues such as substance abuse or domestic issues. Through prayer and careful research, find what works for you and capitalize on those congregants. Remember, each church has an ethos, a way of thinking or a theme unique to itself.

The Purpose of Christian Music

Music is an essential part of the worship experience, but should never overshadow the preached Word. Music is a most powerful method of bringing honor and glory to God. It is also very emotive and can be filled with pitfalls. Few things can divide a church more than issues arising from music selection, leadership and performance.

As such, be mindful of these important musical priorities. Your music and music ministry should:
1. Praise God and inspire the people.
2. Express theological beliefs and sing the Gospels by the leading of the Holy Spirit.
3. Coincide with and support the preached Word.
4. Be based on a foundation and atmosphere of peace between the pastor and the minister of music.
5. Work from a sincere attitude of cooperation and mutual respect between the pastor, music staff and song leaders.
6. Minister to and inspire the congregation.
7. Be planned and properly implemented.[31]

Music Speaks to the Soul God Created in Each of Us.

We are made in the image and likeness of God (Genesis 1:26) and we are spiritual beings having a human experience.

Before I formed you in the womb I knew you, before you were born I set you apart; I appointed you as a prophet to the nations. – Jeremiah 1:5. Yes, God knew us and then formed us. We were spirit first and then manifested into the physical. We are designed by our Creator as relational beings who need fellowship. We are hardwired to engage in community.

There is no doubt that music is an essential part of our God-given humanity and desire to connect with others. We identify ourselves with the music we hold near and dear to our hearts. This is why people now pay thousands of dollars for tickets to see reunions of the rock bands they most loved during their youth.

Music brings us together, as God intended. It was never His intent to have music divide us, yet it does. Any overview of Christian musical history or assessment of music in American churches shows deep division in all four musical criteria of instrumentation, style, text, or "good fruit." (Matthew 7:17-20)

What worshippers find to be acceptable instrumentation varies widely between churches and denominations. Thousands of Christian musical styles have been created, argued over, embraced, rejected, rediscovered, and re-embraced for 2,000 years. The evolution of Christian music and the debates surrounding Christian musical expression will certainly continue. However, we must find some common ground in order to measure the worthiness of the music offered in our churches.

Even the "good fruit" criteria is problematic, for some music may benefit one Christian, yet harm another. Thus, the music could be said to bear both good and bad fruit. For the most part, Christians have agreed only on the criteria of text: words should be

Biblically based or in accord with Christian doctrine and theology.

The Christian musical experience should be characterized as true, noble, just, pure, etc. (Philippians 4:8). However, the cultural manifestation of these qualities are extraordinarily different due to the "Babelization" of the world (Genesis 11) and cultural or historical traditions. For instance, some early American churches forbade instruments during times of worship, even referring to the organ as "the devil's bagpipe." Today, of course, musical instruments are a vital part of worship in the vast majority of Christian churches, with the Eastern Orthodox being the largest exception.

The point of agreement comes with the knowledge that we all seek to worship God in spirit and in truth (John 4:24). Each tradition is, of course, free to express its worship of Jesus as it exhibits the worthy qualities noted by Paul in Philippians 4:8.

There is one caveat, however. Although the character of God is true, noble, just, etc., above all God is a *Redeemer*. There are times in which God will use the ugly, despised, and cursed to bring about His plan and purpose. He took the cursed serpent of Genesis 3 and lifted it up as a symbol of healing for the Israelites in Numbers 21. Likewise, God took the curse of the cross and transformed it into a great symbol of salvation (Galatians 3:13-14).

It is not beyond the power of God to transform and to redeem people through music normally associated with debased and degenerate practices. In these instances, in fact, His greatest mercy is shown.[32]

Your Christian music selections should usher people into the very Presence of God. That is why we assemble. Do not dread the musical process, as so many have come to do. Enjoy it. Have fun selecting your music, your instrumentation, your style, and above all, your lyrical content.

"Even the choicest words lose their power, when they are used to overpower."
- *Edwin Friedman*

Scripture Reading

The Bible states in John 1:1 that Jesus is the *logos* or the written Word of God. Therefore, it is imperative that you always use the Word of God and base your every action on its validity. Scripture may be assigned to members of the congregation to read at the pulpit, or they may be read spontaneously. Be selective on who you choose. This person may be the only Bible your congregants ever read, meaning, he or she is a representative of the public's opinion of God's Word *and* your entire church, just by their reading performance. Make sure the person can pronounce difficult Bible names and has had sufficient practice.

Scripture should be read with power and confidence. Also, the selected reading should align with the sermon being preached. If Scriptures are assigned in advance, make sure your church uses the entire Bible.

Do not select readings exclusively from the New Testament simply because these writings are typically more familiar to your congregants.

Certain members may be asked to quote memorized Scriptures calling attention to some aspect of the person and work of Jesus Christ. The worship leader may wish to acknowledge that these Scriptures are the inspired Word of God, demanding our undivided attention. Some traditions call for the congregation to stand at the reading of the Word. Also, these words from the Bible have the power of God through the Holy Spirit to convey truth, correction, and the assurance of the eternal life. [33]

Most Christians never read their Bible outside of church. So when you have an opportunity to read Scripture aloud during a worship service, you are providing all the Scripture most people will hear that week. This makes Scripture reading a critically important part of any worship experience. Too often we think of the public reading of Scripture as a perfunctory part of the service or as a fill-in between the offering and the sermon. That is tragic, because Scripture reading has always been a cornerstone of worship among Christians (1 Timothy 4:13) and it is always an opportunity for God to speak.

Your Bible reading opportunity can become the high moment of the worship service, a time when God speaks powerfully to people. **Here is what you can do to make that happen:**

1. Pray for God to Speak. Pray that God uses your reading to impact someone's life. Remember, *"The word of God is living and active. Sharper than any double-edged sword,* *it penetrates even to dividing soul and spirit, joints and marrow; it judges the thoughts and attitudes of the heart."* – Hebrews 4:12

2. Use the Congregation's Preferred Translation. Many congregations have a preferred translation of the Bible, either in the pew or projected on a screen. Always use this preferred translation.

3. Practice Reading Aloud. Practice reading several times aloud. Just relax and read with expression. Grasp the meaning, emphasizing the important words or phrases. When you read it like you mean it, people engage at a higher level and learn more from the reading.

4. Here are some tips:

- Read slowly, clearly, and in a strong voice.
- Hold your Bible, tablet or smartphone at chin height so you can read without bending your head down.
- If your Bible has small print, you may want to print your passage in larger print and tape it inside your Bible.
- Use facial expression. This will transfer into vocal expression subconsciously.
- Alter the pitch, rate, and volume of your voice to communicate emotions.
- Find the impact words in the passage and give them special emphasis. For example, "He is patient with you, not wanting anyone to perish but *everyone* to come to repentance." (2 Peter 3:9)
- Pause to show special emphasis. For example, "Then Nathan said to David . . . "*You* are the man!" (2 Samuel 2:17)
- Look up and make eye contact with the audience occasionally. This will help them connect with

you and with the Word.

5. Be Sure You Know All the Words. If there are words you cannot pronounce, listen to the audio at BibleGateway.com. There is also an audio pronunciation guide at NetMinistries.org/resources.

6. Wear the Right Clothing. Dress modestly so that the Word is the star, not you. If you will be using a lapel microphone or wireless headset, wear something that includes a waistband, belt, or pocket so you will have a place to clip the battery pack.

7. Arrive Early. As a Scripture reader, you are a leader in worship for the day. Arrive in plenty of time to consult with the pastor or worship leader, check in with the sound technician if needed, and join the worship team for prayer if that is their custom. Prepare your heart to lead God's people in worship.

8. Move Into Position Quickly. The Scripture reader is generally not introduced, so be in position in order to quickly move to the platform or lectern and begin. It may be appropriate to begin moving into position even before the previous speaker or song has concluded so there is no gap in the service.

9. Introduce the Passage. Say a brief word of introduction before you read to provide context for the passage. It might be as simple as saying, "Today's Scripture is taken from Paul's second letter to the Christians living in the ancient Greek city of Corinth," or it could be lengthier, if the congregation needs more detail in order to understand what they are hearing. At the very least, announce the book, chapter, and verse, then give everyone a moment to find the text in their Bibles so they can read along.

10. Close with an Affirmation. After you have finished reading the passage, say something that encourages people to take the words to heart. **Consider these phrases:**

- ❏ "The Word of the Lord."
- ❏ "This is the Word of God to us."
- ❏ "May God bless the reading of His Word."
- ❏ "May God help us to apply these words to our lives."
- ❏ "Let's not just be hearers of the Word. Let's do it!"[34]

Intercessory Prayer

What is intercessory prayer? It is simply praying to God on behalf of another person, intervening for them. The pastor may lead the congregation in prayer for individual needs within the local fellowship of believers, Christians and ministries around the world, and people or situations outside the faith. As an intercessor you may, on occasion, call on anyone who desires to offer spontaneous prayers. The pastor may also lead a time of directed prayer, asking people to pray silently or audibly for specific needs, which can be announced one by one.

Be careful at this point. For the initiated, directed prayer can be an effective change of pace. However, for new people or visitors, it can be awkward and meaningless.[35]

The Offering

The offering, frequently regarded by some as an inconvenient interruption, is an important part of congregational worship. First and foremost, a person must offer him or herself to God preceding any monetary gift.

The tithe is 10% of the believer's gross income and is the First Fruits (Deuteronomy 18:4, Proverbs 3:9, Romans 11:16) of their daily labor, as a love gift to God and His Kingdom work. The corporate reception of tithes and offerings at a given point in the worship service can and should be a fitting act of worship. Some churches choose even to place the offering immediately after the sermon as a congregational response to God's Word.

Of course, there are many valid methods and traditions of receiving the offering. Some churches place an offerings receptacle in a position that makes it convenient for worshippers to give their gifts as they enter or exit the sanctuary. However it is conducted, the spirit of the offering must be done so with God's grace as the standard.

The argument against tithing usually sounds like this: "I don't have to tithe 10% because I am under grace, not Law." It does not take much effort to draw out the flaw in this logic, because the Law also says: do not murder. But Jesus says do not even be angry with your brother (Matthew 5:21) because this is a higher standard. The Law says: do not commit adultery. But Jesus said to not even look lustfully at a woman (Matthew 5:27). Again, a higher standard. Grace (who is Jesus) is always a higher standard. Grace always exceeds the righteousness of the Law. When you truly realize that Jesus died in your place, you will give more than 10% out of the gratitude of your heart, not your head. Remember, the Bible says that Jesus actually receives the tithe, not the church (Hebrews 7:8).

Two of the results of tithing are:
1. The tithe blesses God's people.
2. The tithe brings provision into God's house.

Tithing becomes an extraordinary opportunity for blessing and abundance for those with the faith to completely trust an unchanging, eternal God. The offering is out of worship for who God is. Tithes belong to Him and are brought out of our response for what He has done. You do not give tithes, you *return* tithes, because they belong to God. Tithing opens the floodgates of heaven (Malachi 3:10), and are the foundation upon which giving is built. Most importantly, tithing removes the curse from your finances.[36]

Offertory Prayers

Offertory prayers should always be directed towards God, asking His help to put His money to good use to build up the Kingdom. After all, it truly is all of His money. He was the One who gave us the wisdom and health to make wealth (Deuteronomy 8:18).

Some offertory prayers include, but are not limited to:

Offertory Prayer Sample #1
Father, we praise you and thank you for these gifts that we have freely given. You said in your Word that you love a cheerful giver. Use them for the upbuilding and glory of your Kingdom. May we remember that every good and perfect gift comes from You. Make this money to be a blessing to those in need, for we seek to honor you in all we think, say and do, in Jesus' name, Amen.

Offertory Prayer Sample #2
O' Lord our heavenly Father, who has freely given us all things through Jesus Christ, accept now these gifts we bring, and give us your grace, that we may yield ourselves completely unto you. Use our gifts and our abilities to the honor of your Kingdom, in Jesus' name we pray, Amen.

Offertory Prayer Sample #3
Gracious Father, as you have freely given us all things, we now freely give unto you ourselves and the substance of our hands. Accept these gifts as a gesture of our sincere worship for you, in the name of Jesus Christ our Lord we pray, Amen. [37]

Benedictions

A benediction is a declaration of blessings from God upon His loved ones. Benedictions, though brief, offer words of assurance or precepts designed to bring joy, peace, comfort, and security to those who place their trust in God, thereby encouraging believers in their commitment to God.

Benedictions from Scripture are often read or recited near the close of a worship service. In this context, benedictions embody a call to unity, faith, and discipleship among the congregation.

Additionally, many believers find meditating on benedictions during their quiet times is a soothing balm which deepens the spirit, provides succor for the ailing heart, and strengthens the faltering soul. Benedictions can be a remarkable source of healing because the words themselves are life (John 6:63). [38]

Benediction Samples:

#1 - The Lord bless you and keep you. The Lord make His face to shine upon you, and be gracious unto you. The Lord lift up His countenance upon you, and give you peace. (Numbers 6:24-26)

#2 - Grace be unto you, and peace, from God our Father and from the Lord Jesus Christ. (1 Corinthians 1:3)

#3 - The grace of the Lord Jesus Christ, and the love of God, and the sweet communion of the Holy Spirit be with you all, Amen. (2 Corinthians 13:14)

#4 - The peace of God which passes all understanding, shall keep your hearts and minds through Christ Jesus our Lord. Now unto God our Father, be glory forever and ever, Amen. (Philippians 4:7, 20)

#5 - Now, the God of peace, that brought again from the dead our Lord Jesus, that great shepherd of the sheep, through the blood of the everlasting covenant, make you perfect in every good work to do His will, working in you that which is well pleasing in His sight, through Jesus Christ, to whom be glory forever and ever, Amen. (Hebrews 13:20-21)

#6 - Now unto Him that is able to keep you from falling, and to present you faultless before the presence of His glory with exceeding joy, to the only wise God our Savior, be glory and majesty, dominion and power, both now and forever, Amen. (Jude 24-25)

#7 - The grace of our Lord Jesus Christ be with you all, Amen. (Revelation 22:21)[39]

#8 - Grace and peace to you from God our Father and the Lord Jesus Christ, who gave Himself for our sins to rescue us from this present evil age, according to the will of our God and Father, to whom be glory, forever and ever, Amen. (Galatians 1:3-5)

#9 - Now to Him who is able to do immeasurably more than all we ask or imagine, according to His power that is at work within us, to Him be glory in the church and in Jesus Christ throughout all generations, forever and ever, Amen. (Ephesians 3:20-21)

#10 - May God Himself, the God of peace, sanctify you through and through. May your whole spirit, soul and body be kept blameless at the coming of our Lord Jesus Christ, Amen. (1 Thessalonians 5:23)

Never forget, the One who spoke, still speaks, and the One who came, will come again, Amen.
— *Max Lucado*

Examples of Church Service Liturgies

Below are two examples of worship services. The arrangement of the elements can vary according to congregational appeal, culture, seasons, function, and formality, but the content will remain mostly unchanged.

First, free worship or contemporary worship creates a less formal atmosphere. This may be a weekday or Saturday night service or an outdoor public worship, or even at a small house church. This type of format appeals to the unchurched who are seeking liberty in Jesus or are just curious. There is usually more music at free worship.

Secondly, formal worship has its place amongst traditional and orthodox churches. The members of this service are more seasoned and want continuity and familiarity. Formal worship may also be appropriate when a pastor is installed or when dignitaries are present. Either way, both free worship and formal worship attempt to focus the attention of the congregants on connecting with God.

Free Worship:

Musical Prelude to Worship – The music played prior

to the beginning of worship sets the tone and atmosphere in the sanctuary for the experience of worshipping God.

Baptism (more on this in the next chapter)

Prayer of Invocation or Call to Worship – Prayer, Scriptures, responsive readings, or songs calling on the Spirit of God to commune with the people, usually conducted by the minister or designee, establishes the purpose and direction of worship.

Scripture – This is simply a reading directly from the Bible, the Word of God (1 Timothy 4:13). The day's reading of Scripture should coincide with the sermon. May be read by: the pastor, associate minister, ministry leader, the congregation in unison, or any designee.

Praise for His Providential Care – We give thanks to the Lord through singing, clapping, dancing, raising of hands, shouting, and an attitude of gratitude for what God has done and for who He is.

Public Prayer – A prayer for the people.

Welcome Visitors – It is extremely important to thank visitors for coming to your church. Please keep in mind that most surveys recommend allowing visitors to remain anonymous. For the most part, they do not like to stand out or be pointed out. You may choose to give them a name card, but even this may feel awkward to the visitor. The best strategy for visitors is making sure you give them a reason to come back and an easy way to show a voluntary interest in becoming a part of your church.

Pastoral Remarks – As the leader of your church, you may consider taking a few moments just to share what's on your mind, greet people, or bring special news. This will allow the congregation to connect with you as a person not just a presider over the worship service.

Communion – Partaking of the elements: wine & bread, the body & blood of Jesus.

Special Presentations – In the life of an active church, there are many moving parts, many of which merit recognition or focus. It is refreshing to experience awards, graduations, certificates, thanks to an outstanding congregant, or new artistic expressions of faith such as drama or puppets.

Performed Worship Music – Performed music is presented to set the mood and inspire the church while invoking the Spirit of God. Choirs, Bands, Praise Teams, call them what you like, they are there to lift up Jesus through the well-chosen, well-rehearsed music focusing hearts and minds on the Lord, NOT the performers.

Corporate Worship Music – This music is participatory, inviting the entire the congregation to sing, clap, move, and experience praising Jesus through song. (Tithes and offerings could go here as well.)

Sermon – Preaching the Word of God is arguably the most important function while serving in the ministry. You are calling people to God, just as Jesus did during His time with us. For now, He is calling on you to speak His Gospel for Him. Make sure the sermon has an application; in other words, it moves the listener to take action that leads to inner transformation.

Intercessory Prayer – These are prayers on behalf of someone who needs deliverance from some oppressive spirit or condition. Suffering people may also be seeking physical, spiritual, emotional, psychological, or financial healing. Prayer intercessors are called by God and can be the heartbeat of the church.

Invitation to Accept Christ – Call people to the altar from their seats to give their lives to Christ.

Offertory Prayer – Prayer over the offering.

Tithes and Offerings

Doxology – (Optional, some use this) Praise God from whom all blessings flow, praise Him all creatures here below, praise Him above ye heavenly host, praise Father, Son and Holy Ghost.

Benediction – A blessing, closing prayer and remarks.

Formal Worship:

Preparation – An appropriate prelude of hymns and Gospel songs will help to set the tone of the service.

Announcements – Announcements should be taken seriously. These events are often the ties that bind the Body of Christ together.

Call to Worship – Prayer, Scripture, responsive reading, or song that calls on the Spirit of God to commune with the people, done by the minister or designee.

Hymn of Praise – The opening hymn should speak to the nature or attributes of God and should be addressed to Him.

Ascriptions of Praise – These may be personal, planned witness statements or the pastor may use the Scripture selections in keeping with the theme of the day.

Prayer of Invocation – This may be a brief prayer in the pastor's own words invoking the manifest presence of God into the worship experience.

Old Testament Scripture – The pastor or designee will choose a passage supportive of the theme of the worship service.

Music – This could be a choral anthem or solo.

Tithes and Offerings – Worshippers are given the opportunity to present their tithes and offerings to God. An instrumental or vocal piece may accompany the reception of the offering.

Doxology and Prayer of Dedication - (Optional, some use this) Praise God from whom all blessings flow, praise Him all creatures here below, praise Him above ye heavenly host, praise Father, Son and Holy Ghost.

New Testament Scripture – The pastor or designee will choose a passage supportive of the theme of the worship service.

Pastoral Prayer – The pastoral prayer is an opportunity for the minister, pastor, or priest to bear before God the praises of His people as well as to intercede for those members with particular needs. Carefully carried out, it can be a highlight of the service and a lasting benediction for the worshippers.

Special Music – A song well executed and appropriate to the theme of the service can prepare the congregation for what follows and permit the pastor a brief time of quiet worship before they stand to minister the Word to the people.

Sermon – The preached Word of God (same as above).

Sermonic Response – This response may be a corporate recitation of the Apostles Creed, a litany prepared and/or printed in the bulletin or on the big screen to a public confession of faith or of dedication.

Hymn of Affirmation – Traditional song supportive of the sermon theme.

Prayer of Thanksgiving – Thanking God for His grace and mercy.

Pastoral Charge – The pastor, minister, or priest in his or her charge to the congregation may repeat the major theme of the worship time.

Benediction – A blessing, closing prayer, and remarks.

Postlude – Congregation may sing a chorus or the organist may play a selection.[40]

Baptism

Water Baptism

While Baptism is essential to the Christian experience, few traditions agree on even its basic issues. For centuries, disagreements over how and where baptism should be conducted, who is eligible, and its place in salvation have caused great division among believers.

It seems the only point upon which we can all agree is that baptism is vitally important and we must do it. It is ironic and sad that so much division takes place over one doctrine. Baptism is one of only two ordinances (Baptism and The Lord's Supper) common in most every Christian church.

Dr. Martyn Lloyd Jones, former Minister at Westminster Chapel in London, an innovative and wise man of God, provides incredible clarity on Baptism from his book, *Great Doctrines of the Bible*.

What is baptism? The word baptism comes from the Greek word *"baptizo"* which means to be completely immersed. By total immersion (body being totally submerged in water) or partial immersion (water poured over one's head, or dunking of one's head into water) or the sprinkling of water (on top of head or forehead), God has chosen to signify and seal us to our redemption, our forgiveness, the remission of our sins, our union with Christ, our being baptized into Him, and our receiving of the Holy Spirit.

Some traditions or denominations consider the sprinkling baptism or christening of a child complete. While others say the child must be baptized when they reach the age of accountability. Regardless, the person must know for themselves in their heart they have received the death of Jesus Christ and His shed blood as payment for their sins and have accepted Him as their personal Lord and Savior. Then, the act of baptism takes on meaning and relevance. Baptism is an outward gesture of an inward transformation. Its significance is not in the mode or method of baptism, but in what has happened by faith to the believer.

What does baptism teach us? Baptism teaches us we are in union. We are placed into something. We are baptized into the Holy Spirit, into Christ, into the Trinity, into the Body and unto Moses. We are cleansed and purified. We are cleansed from the guilt of sin (Acts 22:16).

What is the function of Baptism?
- ❏ It is a sign and seal of the remission of our sins and justification.
- ❏ It is a sign and seal of our regeneration, of our union with Christ and our receiving of the indwelling Holy Spirit.
- ❏ God gave the rainbow, so He gives us a sign and seal of our regeneration in the act of Baptism.
- ❏ It is a seal for the believer. It is not something we do, it is something that is done to us and within us.
- ❏ It is a bearing of our witness and testimony that

we believe the truth. We believe something has already happened to us; we are saved, passed from death to life.

❑ It is something that can be seen, so it seals us to the promise of forgiveness.

Baptism is by God's appointment, whatever the mode, let us remember we are sealed.[41]

On top of all of this, Jesus was baptized and if you claim you are His child, you too should be baptized.

Then Jesus came from Galilee to the Jordan to be baptized by John. But John tried to deter him, saying, "I need to be baptized by you, and do you come to me?" Jesus replied, "Let it be so now; it is proper for us to do this to fulfill all righteousness." Then John consented. As soon as Jesus was baptized, he went up out of the water. At that moment heaven was opened, and he saw the Spirit of God descending like a dove and lighting on him. And a voice from heaven said, "This is my Son, whom I love; with him I am well pleased." – Matthew 3:14-17

Baptism does not wash away our sins. Your sins were dealt with when you received Christ. His shed blood took away all your sins, past, present and future. How do we know this? Jesus Himself was baptized and He knew no sin. He was the sinless Lamb of God. Jesus was baptized to fulfill all righteousness, to obey the will of His Father. It is the Father's will that if we profess to be His child and we are a Christian, then we should also be baptized. What was the Father's reaction to Jesus' baptism? The Father spoke from heaven and said He is well pleased and loves His Son Jesus. Very simply, since we too have Jesus, our Baptism pleases God.

Water Baptism Services

For people to grasp the true meaning of what baptism does for the believer, it would be very advantageous to your church and your congregants to have a baptism class in which the doctrine of baptism is explained. During this class it is very helpful for those baptism candidates to tell you their personal testimony of their conversion experience. You cannot baptize anyone who has not received Jesus as their personal Lord and Savior. When candidates receive Jesus Christ, baptism actually becomes a public confession. The Apostle Paul said in Romans chapter 6:5, *If we have been united with him [Jesus] like this in his death, we will certainly also be united with him in his resurrection.*

Your baptism service liturgy could be the same as your Sunday worship service. The actual baptism could be placed right after the musical prelude or anywhere after the invocation, welcome, pastoral remarks and/or Communion. The baptism is typically a visible witness to the regeneration that has already taken place in the heart of the believer who has accepted Christ. It is a symbolic representation of Christ being submerged in the grave for three days, so the candidates are also submerged. The baptism confers our membership in the Body of Christ, the Christian community.

For those who view baptism as a personal testimony or acceptance into the covenant relationship of Christ, baptism should be performed before a worshipping congregation, whether inside or outside. River, pond, ocean, or swimming pool baptisms are excellent ways to expose the public to Jesus. Baptism signifies that to be a Christian one must be adopted, nurtured, loved, and guided by a church family. Baptism is most effective when it is made clear that it is an act of the whole congregation. Baptism is nothing less than the birth and creation of the church, created anew in each generation by the loving, powerful act of God.

The baptismal service should accomplish five things:
1. **Initiation** – a public declaration of faith.
2. **Celebration** – a joyous public event.
3. **Instruction** – people should learn what baptism means along with its significance (Romans 6:3-7).
4. **Proclamation** – what baptism means to the non-Christians present.
5. **Invitation** – the Holy Spirit is powerful at this moment. It would be a great time to have an invitation to accept Christ.

Step-By-Step: Full Immersion Baptism

Right before the actual baptism, candidates, deacons, and helpers witness and/or practice the immersion experience out of water. This relaxes nerves. Prayer is performed for the entire gathering of candidates and their families. Next, each candidate and their family members partake of the Lord's Supper. In addition, some last minute instructions may be given for special needs or special circumstances.

The minister then enters the water, followed by the candidates. While the candidate is in the water at waist level, the baptizing minister, while looking at the candidate, says out loud, **"(name of candidate), by your profession of faith in the Lord Jesus Christ, I now baptize you in the name of the Father and of the Son and of the Holy Spirit."**

Just prior to immersion, the candidate can either hold their nose or the minister will place a white wash cloth over their nose. This keeps water from backing up the candidate's nose. The easiest way to baptize a person is to have the candidate fold their arms across their chest. The minister, with one hand behind the neck and the other holding onto their folded arms, lowers the person backwards under the water. Then the person is lifted back up to a standing position.

Some ministers, as they are lowering the person, under the water say, "Buried in the likeness of His death," and when they stand the person up say, "Raised in the likeness of His resurrection." When the person walks out of the water they say, "To walk in newness of life." [46]

Suggested Baptism Scriptures:

(Matthew 3:13-17) *Then Jesus came from Galilee to the Jordan to be baptized by John. But John tried to deter him, saying, "I need to be baptized by you, and do you come to me?" Jesus replied, "Let it be so now; it is proper for us to do this to fulfill all righteousness." Then John consented. As soon as Jesus was baptized, he went up out of the water. At that moment heaven was opened, and he saw the Spirit of God descending like a dove and lighting on him. And a voice from heaven said, "This is my Son, whom I love; with him I am well pleased."*

(Matthew 28:18-20) *Then Jesus came to them and said, "All authority in heaven and on earth has been given to me. Therefore go and make disciples of all nations, baptizing them in the name of the Father and of the Son and of the Holy Spirit, and teaching them to obey everything I have commanded you. And surely I am with you always, to the very end of the age."*

(Mark 1:4) *And so John the Baptist appeared in the wilderness, preaching a baptism of repentance for the forgiveness of sins.*

(Mark 1:7-8) *And this was his message: "After me comes the one more powerful than I, the straps of whose sandals I am not worthy to stoop down and untie. I baptize you with water, but he will baptize you with the Holy Spirit."*

(Acts 2:38-41) *Peter replied, "Repent and be baptized, every one of you, in the name of Jesus Christ for the forgiveness of your sins. And you will receive the gift of the Holy Spirit. The promise is for you and your children and for all who are far off—for all whom the Lord our God will call." With many other words he warned them; and he pleaded with them, "Save yourselves from this corrupt generation." Those who accepted his message were baptized, and about three thousand were added to their number that day.*

(Romans 6:3-5) *Or don't you know that all of us who were baptized into Christ Jesus were baptized into his death? We were therefore buried with him through baptism into death in order that, just as Christ was raised from the dead through the glory of the Father, we too may live a new life. For if we have been united with him in a death like his, we will certainly also be united with him in a resurrection like his.*

(Romans 6:8-12) *Now if we died with Christ, we believe that we will also live with him. For we know that since Christ was raised from the dead, he cannot die again; death no longer has mastery over him. The death he died, he died to sin once for all; but the life he lives, he lives to God. In the same way, count yourselves dead to sin but alive to God in Christ Jesus. Therefore do not let sin reign in your mortal body so that you obey its evil desires.*

(Galatians 3:26-27) *So in Christ Jesus you are all children of God through faith, for all of you who were baptized into Christ have clothed yourselves with Christ.* (Colossians 2:12) *Having been buried with him in baptism, in which you were also raised with him through your faith in the working of God, who raised him from the dead.*

(Colossians 3:1-3) *Since, then, you have been raised with Christ, set your hearts on things above, where Christ is, seated at the right hand of God. Set your minds on things above, not on earthly things. For you died, and your life is now hidden with Christ in God.*

(Luke 3:21-22) *When all the people were being baptized, Jesus was baptized too. And as he was praying, heaven was opened and the Holy Spirit descended on him in bodily form like a dove. And a voice came from heaven: "You are my Son, whom I love; with you I am well pleased."*

Sample Baptismal Service:

Music Selection
(Baptism Can Take Place Here)
Invocation or Call to Worship
Scripture
Public Prayer
Welcome Visitors
Pastoral Remarks
Communion
Special Presentations
(Baptism Can Take Place Here)
Worship Music
Sermon
Invitation to Accept Christ
Intercessory Prayer
Tithes and Offerings
Benediction

Baptism in the Holy Spirit

What is the Baptism in the Holy Spirit? The Baptism of the Holy Spirit is when the believer is endued and filled with the power and presence of the Lord for service and to exalt Christ. It happens at the moment we accept Christ. In an instant we are regenerated, made new and declared not guilty before a holy God (2 Corinthians 5:17). It is a gateway into the supernatural. A supernatural infilling and a supernatural overflowing. The Holy Spirit Baptism brings about unity in the Body of Christ. Through it, you are brought into the fullness of Christ.

It is found in Scripture, Matthew 3: 11, Acts 1:5 *"I baptize you with water for repentance. But after me comes one who is more powerful than I, whose sandals I am not worthy to carry. He will baptize you with the Holy Spirit and fire."* – Matthew 3:11

"For John baptized with water, but in a few days you will be baptized with the Holy Spirit." – Acts 1:5

How do you obtain the Baptism in the Holy Spirit? You must:
1. Want it.
2. Ask God for it.
3. Believe He can give you this power.
4. Receive it.

The indwelling, filling, and Baptism of the Holy Spirit refers to the Spirit's taking up permanent residence in the life of believers which continues throughout their lives here on earth. The Bible shows us that Baptism in the Holy Spirit only happens once, at the moment of conversion (Ephesians 4:5). True, yet we leak. Life wears you down, pollutes us and we start to become more worldly (James 1:27). As believers, we must go back to the filling station of the Holy Spirit from time to time and be refilled. The filling of the

Holy Spirit refers to His control and empowerment in believers to enable us to live the victorious Christian life (Ephesians 5:18-20). A continuous or repeated action means the believer needs to be refilled (Acts 2:4; 4:8, 31). To surrender means the believer brings their will, mind, emotions and actions into the place of obedience, conformity and direction to the Holy Spirit of God.

The characteristics of Spirit-filling is a Christ-like character and spiritual fruit – Galatians 5:22, 23:

- **Love** - self-giving, self-sacrificing, caring for and seeking good for others.
- **Joy** - gladness of heart.
- **Peace** - quietness of heart and mind.
- **Patience** - endurance, long suffering, forbearance, slow to anger.
- **Kindness** - unselfish concern for the welfare of others and a desire to be helpful even at great personal sacrifice.
- **Goodness** - performing beneficial acts for others, benevolence.
- **Faithfulness** - loyalty, commitment, trustworthiness and honesty.
- **Gentleness** - restraint coupled with strength and courage, meekness and humility.
- **Self-Control** - self-restraint, continence, mastering one's own desires and practices.

Christians must practice these virtues over and over again throughout their lives. They will never discover a law prohibiting them from living according to these principles. No one needs to know the Word of God more than a person who has just been baptized in the Holy Spirit. Take up the Sword of the Spirit (Ephesians 6:17) along with the Gifts of the Holy Spirit (1 Corinthians chapter 12) and complete your ministry according to God's will.

The Baptism in the Holy Spirit places us in Christ (Romans 8:14- 17), which enables us to receive power. It is the work of the Holy Spirit that joins believers by faith to the Body of Christ. It is the Holy Spirit which brings us into Christ. The Baptism in the Holy Spirit occurs only once in a believer's life and points to the consecrating of the believer to God's work of witnessing in power and righteousness. The nature of Spirit Baptism is unique (Colossians 2: 9, 10) and it is universal (Galatians 3:26-29). When one is baptized in the Holy Spirit, you will have the Holy Spirit without measure, limitless (Acts 2). God has complete control over your life and you have power to do the greater works Jesus talked about (John 14:12). The Baptism of the Holy Spirit is one of the blessings, while baptism of fire means judgment.[42]

The Seven Purposes of the Spirit Baptism

1. For Witnessing – The Baptism in the Holy Spirit is intended to clothe us with supernatural power from on high for the purpose of witnessing.

But ye shall receive power, after that the Holy Ghost is come upon you: and ye shall be witnesses unto me both in Jerusalem, and in all Judea, and in Samaria, and unto the uttermost part of the earth. (Acts 1:8 KJV)

2. For Prayer – The Baptism in the Holy Spirit increases your prayer life, enabling you to pray in the Spirit.

Praying always with all prayer and supplication in the Spirit, and watching thereunto with all perseverance and supplication for all saints. (Ephesians 6:18 KJV)

3. For Teaching – The Holy Spirit is the great Teacher of the Scriptures. He leads us into all truth and reveals Jesus to us.

But the Counselor, the Holy Spirit, whom the Father will send in my name, will teach you all things and will remind you of everything I have said to you. (John 14:26)

4. To Exalt Christ – The Baptism in the Holy Spirit helps you to exalt Christ. This means you lift Him up to His place of supremacy.

I eagerly expect and hope that I will in no way be ashamed, but will have sufficient courage so that now as always Christ will be exalted in my body, whether by life or by death. (Philippians 1:20)

5. For Guidance – The Baptism in the Holy Spirit gives you supernatural warning and direction in order to survive and thrive in this world.

But when he, the Spirit of truth, comes, he will guide you into all truth. He will not speak on his own; he will speak only what he hears, and he will tell you what is yet to come. (John 16:13)

6. For Health – The life of Jesus is to be made manifest in our mortal body. The Spirit of Jesus is in you, and there is no room for the works of the devil.

We always carry around in our body the death of Jesus, so that the life of Jesus may also be revealed in our body. For we who are alive are always being given over to death for Jesus' sake, so that his life may be revealed in our mortal body. (2 Corinthians 4:10-11)

7. For Unity – The purpose of God baptizing believers in the Holy Spirit is to unite them, not to separate them.

For we were all baptized by one Spirit into one body-whether Jews or Greeks, slave or free-and we were all given the one Spirit to drink. (1 Corinthians 12:13)[43]

Speaking in Tongues

Believers should seek the spiritual gift of speaking in tongues (1 Corinthians 14). Speaking in tongues is the supernatural gateway into the realm of the Holy Spirit. Tongues is a supernatural utterance in an unknown tongue. As ministers, we are to help people see that God gave this gift on Pentecost and it is still available today to everyone who believes.

Remember, it is a gift (1 Corinthians 12:4-11). There is nothing you do to earn it. Just as a person opens their mouth to take a drink, you must open your mouth and desire to receive the gift of the Holy Spirit. Sometimes, it happens with the laying on of hands or during prayer or fasting. This author received the gift of speaking in tongues during a Sunday worship service. Do not limit God or the possibilities of how He may go about fulfilling His will. He can do anything, anytime, anywhere.

Speaking in tongues is Biblically sound. *All of them were filled with the Holy Spirit and began to speak in other tongues as the Spirit enabled them.* – Acts 2:4. "Them" (meaning those speaking in tongues) is the subject of the passage. These people did the talking. The Holy Spirit enabled them or gave them the utterance.

Other Bible passages concerning speaking in tongues are:

While Peter was still speaking these words, the Holy Spirit came on all who heard the message. The circumcised believers who had come with Peter were astonished that the gift of the Holy Spirit had been poured out even on Gentiles. For they heard them speaking in tongues and praising God. – Acts 10:44-46.

I thank God that I speak in tongues more than all of you. – 1 Cor. 14:18. *When Paul placed his hands on them, the Holy Spirit came on them, and they spoke in tongues and prophesied.* – Acts 19:6.

Therefore, it is to be expected that when the candidate receives the Holy Spirit, he or she will speak in tongues as the Spirit gives utterance. The person must want to receive this gift. God will not force this gift on anyone. The Holy Spirit does not speak in tongues. The Holy Spirit does not take hold of our tongues and do the talking for us. We do the speaking, and tongues comes out. Speaking in tongues is men and women in the flesh, worshipping God in the Spirit. *And it shall come to pass afterward, I will pour out my Spirit on all flesh.* – Joel 2:28.

Many people say they heard or felt supernatural words forming inside their inner being and the words bubbled up until they were spoken through their mouth. Some people say they feel their lips moving or a tightening of the jaw or the tongue may feel thick. The Holy Spirit uses the organs to form the words. Those present should pray in the Holy Spirit if they pray out loud, otherwise they should pray quietly in their natural language.

Why should every believer speak in tongues?
1. **Tongues is the initial sign** – It is the initial evidence that the Holy Spirit has indwelt us. (Acts 2:4)
2. **Tongues is for spiritual edification** – *He who*

speaks in a tongue edifies himself, but he who prophesies edifies the church. (1 Corinthians 14:4)

3. **Tongues remind us of the Spirit's indwelling presence** – Continued practice of speaking and praying in tongues helps us to be conscious of the Spirit's presence. (Acts 10:46)
4. **Praying in tongues is praying in line with God's perfect will.** (1 Corinthians 14:4)
5. **Praying in tongues stimulates faith.** (Jude 20)
6. **Praying in tongues is a means of keeping free from worldly contamination.** (1 Corinthians 14:28)
7. **Praying in tongues enables us to pray for the unknown.** (Romans 8:26)
8. **Praying in tongues gives spiritual refreshing.** (Isaiah 28:11-12)
9. **Praying in tongues helps you give thanks perfectly.** (1 Corinthians 14:15-17)
10. **Speaking in tongues brings the tongue under subjection.** (James 3:8)[44]

Speaking in tongues is based on an act of the human will. Every tongue is unique, like a fingerprint. Do not repeat in tongues what other people are speaking. God will give you your own special dialect of tongues to praise Him. The fact that you speak is not supernatural. The supernatural part is what is being said and the place from where it is coming.

How Spiritual Power Is Lost

When a believer receives the Lord Jesus Christ as their Savior, they are filled with the Holy Spirit and receive power (John 1:12 KJV) and sonship. They become privileged children of God, co-heirs with Christ (Romans 8:14-17).

But the power and gifts of God must be used to build God's Kingdom (Ephesians 4:11-13), not tear it down and bring disgrace on God's holy name and character. If the believer is moved with pride, rebellion and selfish motives, their power and/or position may be removed by the One who bestowed it. **Below are some principles with corresponding Scriptures documenting this:**

1. **Separation from God** (Numbers 6:1-8, Judges 13:1-7; 16:15-22).
2. **Incoming of Sin and Transgression** (1 Samuel 8:6-9, 12:12-15, 13:7-15, 15:1-3, 7-29, 2 Samuel 12: 7-10 David's transgression, 12:10-13 David's iniquity begins).
3. **Self-Indulgence** (Galatians 5:17, 1 Corinthians 9:27, James 1:13- 15).
4. **Greed for money** (1 Timothy 6:10, Hebrews 13:5).
5. **Pride** (1 Peter 5:5).
6. **Neglect of Prayer** (Ephesians 6:18, neglect of the Word, 2 Timothy 2:15).[45]

The Lord's Supper or Communion

What It Is

In the ordinance of *Communion* or the *Lord's Supper*, believers experience the most blessed and sacred bond between themselves, their risen Lord, and one another. Jesus Himself instituted the supper in Matthew 26:26-30, therefore the most appropriate name is the Lord's Supper.[43] This special part of the worship service memorializes the atoning death of Jesus Christ. His death literally reconciled us back to the Father and perpetuates the Gospel of His redeeming grace. It is a worship celebration, a thanksgiving for Christ's gift to us, our eternal salvation, and is an acknowledgement of His living presence during the act of worship.

While some churches practice open communion, meaning the adults make their own decision whether to take part in Communion, only those who are saved should partake of the elements. Be very careful here, as it is up to the pastor's discretion. This is the Lord's Table, not yours. As the pastor, priest or minister you should understand the sacredness of the moment at hand, explaining the holy significance within the experience to each participant every time it is observed. Paul said, *"So then, whoever eats the bread or drinks the cup of the Lord in an unworthy manner will be guilty*

of sinning against the body and blood of the Lord. Everyone ought to examine themselves before they eat of the bread and drink from the cup. For those who eat and drink without discerning the body of Christ eat and drink judgment on themselves. That is why many among you are weak and sick, and a number of you have fallen asleep. But if we were more discerning with regard to ourselves, we would not come under such judgment."
– 1 Corinthians 11:27-31

Here is an effective way of explaining the Lord's Supper, Communion, Sacraments, or the Eucharist: the elements of bread and wine taken together with the Holy Spirit, represent Jesus. The reason we partake is to commemorate Jesus and His commune with us. The focus is on Him, the act is holy and in the presence of God. The Lord's Supper is a command - *"Do this in remembrance of me."* – 1 Corinthians 11:24

The church received this command to continually administer the Lord's Supper until He returns. Some churches have Communion weekly. Other churches take it monthly, quarterly or twice annually. Furthermore, the Lord's Supper is a wonderful way to commune with others at church retreats or other times of fellowship. Regardless of how much you partake of this Holy Communion, the Apostle Paul said, *"For whenever you eat this bread and drink this cup, you proclaim the Lord's death until He comes."* – 1 Corinthians 11:26

Emphasis on the Lord's Supper

There is a threefold emphasis in the Lord's Supper as instituted by Jesus according to Paul in First Corinthians 11:23-26:
- ❏ The bread symbolizes His broken body.
- ❏ The cup symbolizes His shed blood.
- ❏ At the end of the Lord's Supper, we publicly recognize that we will continue remembering Jesus in this way until He returns.

The Lord's Supper should be one of the most beautiful and holy events in the church.[47]

Remember, the name *Communion* symbolizes the believer's fellowship with Christ and that His presence permeates the elements of bread and wine, as well as the minds and hearts of the believers who are present. No other service in the church reflects the vital elements of Christian experience and faith as does the Lord's Supper.

Preparation for Communion

It will be best if the leader oversees the preparation of the communion table and the elements. If not, leave it in the capable, trusted, and responsible hands of the trained diaconate. If the Lord's Supper is to be administered in a formal setting, candles, clean linens and polished communionware are indispensable. Make sure that all who assist are properly attired and well informed as to what is expected of them and how the service is to proceed.

The Catholic Church believes in transubstantiation, the belief that the bread and wine change into the actual body and blood of Christ. Most Protestant churches practice consubstantiation - the belief that the bread and wine are symbolic of the body and blood of Christ. Regardless, Christ is our Savior and we should be grateful He has died to save us.

Sample Communion Prayer

You or your designee should offer a prayer before the congregation takes the elements. This prayer should be somewhat of a spiritual examination, where each congregant confesses their sins and asks forgiveness. Such as:

O' Lord, we praise you for the gift of your Son Jesus Christ, who died upon the cross. We do not approach this table trusting in our own righteousness, but in your mercy. Forgive our transgressions and sins and cleanse our hearts. Renew in us a right spirit and make us aware of the presence of our living Lord Jesus, in whose name we pray, Amen.[48]

This is also a teaching moment. Here you can apply the principles of what Jesus did on the cross and His death so that the congregation may understand they have been given life and they now have it more abundantly (John 10:10).

Administering Communion

As you hold the bread in your right hand, you can perhaps say something from 1 Corinthians chapter 11 like, *"Jesus said, this is my body, which has been given up for you."* Take and eat. Simultaneous Communion is widely practiced by most churches, meaning everyone takes the elements at the same time, heightening congregational unity. After allowing time for the people to swallow the bread, you can say, "In the same way He also took the cup after supper and said, *'This cup is the new covenant in my blood, do this as often as you drink it, in remembrance of me.'*" Take and drink the cup. Followed by Hallelujah or Amen.

Here, a hymn could be sung or the choir could be singing softly or music played over the sound system. Communion songs should be chosen which lead the congregation through the themes of death, resurrection and celebration. [49]

Communion at the Altar

Many churches customarily serve the elements while participants kneel or stand at the altar. Deacons and ushers may be enlisted to regulate the orderly flow of people to and from the altar, starting from the front according to a prearranged pattern. Aged or infirmed people who find it difficult to kneel may be seated on a front pew to be served. Participants are first served the bread, then the cup while the pastor comments appropriately as the elements are distributed.

Finally, conclude with a brief prayer before dismissing those kneeling in preparation for the next group. The elements may be distributed in total silence or with singing, testimony, or recitation of Scripture. Regardless of your approach, make sure clear instructions have been given so the procedure will operate smoothly. [50]

Suggested Communion Scriptures

#1 - (Matthew 5:3-12*)* *"Blessed are the poor in spirit, for theirs is the Kingdom of heaven.*
4 Blessed are those who mourn,
for they will be comforted.
5 Blessed are the meek,
for they will inherit the earth.
6 Blessed are those who hunger and thirst for righteousness,
for they will be filled.
7 Blessed are the merciful,
for they will be shown mercy.
8 Blessed are the pure in heart, for they will see God.
9 Blessed are the peacemakers,
for they will be called children of God.
10 Blessed are those who are persecuted because of righteousness, for theirs is the Kingdom of heaven.
11 "Blessed are you when people insult you, persecute you and

falsely say all kinds of evil against you because of me. [12] *Rejoice and be glad, because great is your reward in heaven, for in the same way they persecuted the prophets who were before you.*

#2 - (Mark 14:22-26) [22] *While they were eating, Jesus took bread, and when he had given thanks, he broke it and gave it to his disciples, saying, "Take it; this is my body."* [23] *Then he took a cup, and when he had given thanks, he gave it to them, and they all drank from it.* [24] *"This is my blood of the covenant, which is poured out for many," he said to them.* [25] *"Truly I tell you, I will not drink again from the fruit of the vine until that day when I drink it new in the Kingdom of God."* [26] *When they had sung a hymn, they went out to the Mount of Olives.*

#3 - (Luke 22:19-22) [19] *And he took bread, gave thanks and broke it, and gave it to them, saying, "This is my body given for you; do this in remembrance of me."* [20] *In the same way, after the supper he took the cup, saying, "This cup is the new covenant in my blood, which is poured out for you.* [21] *But the hand of him who is going to betray me is with mine on the table.* [22] *The Son of Man will go as it has been decreed. But woe to that man who betrays him!"*

#4 - (John 6:35-40) [35] *Then Jesus declared, "I am the bread of life. Whoever comes to me will never go hungry, and whoever believes in me will never be thirsty.* [36] *But as I told you, you have seen me and still you do not believe.* [37] *All those the Father gives me will come to me, and whoever comes to me I will never drive away.* [38] *For I have come down from heaven not to do my will but to do the will of him who sent me.* [39] *And this is the will of him who sent me that I shall lose none of all those he has given me, but raise them up at the last day.* [40] *For my Father's will is* *that everyone who looks to the Son and believes in him shall have eternal life, and I will raise them up at the last day."*

#5 - (Romans 8:28-30)[28] *And we know that in all things God works for the good of those who love him, who have been called according to his purpose.* [29] *For those God foreknew he also predestined to be conformed to the image of his Son, that he might be the firstborn among many brothers and sisters.* [30] *And those he predestined, he also called; those he called, he also justified; those he justified, he also glorified.*

#6 - (1 Corinthians 11:23-26)[23] *For I received from the Lord what I also passed on to you: The Lord Jesus, on the night he was betrayed, took bread,* [24] *and when he had given thanks, he broke it and said, "This is my body, which is for you; do this in remembrance of me."* [25] *In the same way, after supper he took the cup, saying, "This cup is the new covenant in my blood; do this, whenever you drink it, in remembrance of me."* [26] *For whenever you eat this bread and drink this cup, you proclaim the Lord's death until he comes.*

#7 - (Ephesians 3:20-4:6)[20] *Now to him who is able to do immeasurably more than all we ask or imagine, according to his power that is at work within us,* [21] *to him be glory in the church and in Christ Jesus throughout all generations, forever and ever! Amen. As a prisoner for the Lord, then, I urge you to live a life worthy of the calling you have received.* [2] *Be completely humble and gentle; be patient, bearing with one another in love.* [3] *Make every effort to keep the unity of the Spirit through the bond of peace.* [4] *There is one body and one Spirit, just as you were called to one hope when you were called;* [5] *one Lord, one faith, one baptism,* [6] *one God and Father of all, who is over all and through all and in all.*

#8 - (Philippians 2:1-11) *Therefore if you have any encouragement from being united with Christ, if any comfort from his love, if any common sharing in the Spirit, if any tenderness and compassion,* [2] *then make my joy complete by being like-minded, having the same love, being one in spirit and of one mind.* [3] *Do nothing out of selfish ambition or vain conceit. Rather, in humility value others above yourselves,* [4] *not looking to your own interests but each of you to the interests of the others.*

[5] *In your relationships with one another, have the same mindset as Christ Jesus:*

[6] *Who, being in very nature God,*
did not consider equality with God something to be used to his own advantage;
[7] *rather, he made himself nothing*
by taking the very nature of a servant,
being made in human likeness.
[8] *And being found in appearance as a man,*
he humbled himself
by becoming obedient to death—
even death on a cross!
[9] *Therefore God exalted him to the highest place*
and gave him the name that is above every name,
[10] *that at the name of Jesus every knee should bow,*
in heaven and on earth and under the earth,
[11] *and every tongue acknowledge that Jesus Christ is Lord, to the glory of God the Father.*

#9 - (Revelation 22:14, 17, 20-21) [14] *"Blessed are those who wash their robes, that they may have the right to the tree of life and may go through the gates into the city.* [15] *Outside are the dogs, those who practice magic arts, the sexually immoral, the murderers, the idolaters and everyone who loves and practices* *falsehood.*

¹⁶ *"I, Jesus, have sent my angel to give you this testimony for the churches. I am the Root and the Offspring of David, and the bright Morning Star."*

¹⁷ *The Spirit and the bride say, "Come!" And let the one who hears say, "Come!" Let the one who is thirsty come; and let the one who wishes take the free gift of the water of life.*

¹⁸ *I warn everyone who hears the words of the prophecy of this scroll: If anyone adds anything to them, God will add to that person the plagues described in this*

scroll. ¹⁹ *And if anyone takes words away from this scroll of prophecy, God will take away from that person any share in the tree of life and in the Holy City, which are described in this scroll.*

²⁰ *He who testifies to these things says, "Yes, I am coming soon." Amen. Come, Lord Jesus.*

²¹ *The grace of the Lord Jesus be with God's people. Amen.*

Weddings

Guiding Principles of Marriage

First and foremost, in the mind and heart of the minister, you must realize that a wedding is a worship service. Christ is always to be exalted by the behavior of the minister before, during, and after the ceremony. This is why we often begin the ceremony by stating something akin to, "We come together as a community to worship God through the union of this couple in marriage, reverently and in the fear and witness of God."

The Lord instituted marriage in the Garden (Genesis 2) and it is an image of God's relationship to His people. As such, Holy Matrimony is the only union recognized between a man and a woman. In your conscience and character, you will have to decide as a minister whom you will and will not marry. The Bible says that people should not be unequally yoked (2 Corinthians 6:14). The consequences of this one verse are serious. You must consider the Biblical truth that performing a wedding for a couple in which one or both people do not know Christ could doom the marriage from the beginning.

Of all the varied pastoral ministry privileges, outside of leading people to Christ and baptizing them, two functions stand out as most important: weddings and funerals. Nearly every family in the church will at some time need the pastor for weddings and funerals. Some pastors are involved in a family's life for several generations, marrying parents, adult children, grandchildren, and so on. This means you may become the one source for all faith-filled guidance trusted by all the people in one lineage, giving you the unique opportunity to make disciples through God's grace.[51]

Marriage is the most serious long-term commitment a couple will make in their lifetime, but many enter into it with a lack of maturity and knowledge. Increasing divorce rates make it imperative that people be adequately prepared for marriage. A good marriage might be made in heaven, but the maintenance happens on earth. Love is a fragile commodity which needs to be cultivated and nourished constantly. Those intending to marry should look to God for His guidance, but the success of the marriage largely depends on the couple and their efforts in response to God's leading.

Important guiding principles for couples coming to you for a marriage ceremony:

- ❏ A good marriage is not based on idealism, but on reality. The Cinderella Syndrome in which every girl finds a prince and every boy finds a princess, living happily ever after, is a fairy tale. Far too many couples marry with unrealistically high expectations and then spend years suffering and adjusting.
- ❏ A happy marriage is based on respect for oneself and for the partner. A poor self-image, developed for any reason, can lead to stormy seas. A solid relationship with Jesus Christ and

an understanding of oneself in the light of that relationship are essential to a happy, life-long marriage that honors God.

- ❏ In a good marriage, the couple must have a deep understanding of each other. This "emotional intimacy" keeps the relationship from misunderstanding and conflict. It does not take much discernment to realize that males and females are different physically, but few anticipate or accept how different they are emotionally and mentally.[52]

- ❏ Work and vigilance *after the wedding* are essential. When two people fall in love and decide to get married they begin one of the most rewarding relationships God designed. Many couples make the mistake of believing the powerful, "irresistible" feelings that motivated their decision are enough to secure a healthy marriage. This is not true. The wedding is a sacred event, but the marriage is a separate, equally sacred, journey that must be taken seriously every day.

- ❏ Marriage is something that we must choose anew every morning. Even during the courtship period, couples begin to discover that their feelings of love fluctuate and change. The only way to maintain true love is to realize that love is a choice. Each spouse must wake every day and decide that they will do their utmost to honor God through their marriage

- ❏ A good marriage is based on intentional choice. The decision to marry and maintain a monogamous, loving relationship requires understanding the dynamics of marriage and how all your choices will affect your marriage.

❑ To have an extraordinary marriage, couples must realize there are many factors that influence a happy marriage: Family of origin, communication, conflict resolution, attitudes, religion, financial management, sexual relationship, children, in-laws, even political preference, among many others, must be carefully and pragmatically considered prior to marriage.

❑ Good marriages are built on love, knowledge and understanding of behavioral patterns. The couple will develop a solid relationship over time if their foundation is built on commitment to God, themselves, and each other. These three pillars must be of primary importance to both people.

❑ A lasting marriage happens when both people understand that everything brought into the marriage relationship has been influenced by the couple's family of origin. You are who you are because of what you have experienced, inherited, been taught and witnessed being modeled throughout your life. A comprehensive study on family of origin will shed light and aid both people, especially during conflict.[53]

Relationship Love Types

✝

The English language has many definitions for the word *love*. For your ministry, we will distinguish three types of love: Emotional-love, Friendship-love and Commitment-love.

Emotional-love is the feeling of being "in love," which at many times predominates over rational thought. Our feelings of love are conditional. Consequently, those feelings can change.

Emotions can be ignited like a fire. The more you fan the fire, the more it grows. But a fire quickly flickers and goes out if not attended. Couples who consider being in love as the only basis for marriage will often divorce when their emotions wane. They think they have lost their marriage because they have lost their initial feelings for one another. A marriage based on feelings alone is destined to fail.

We communicate emotional love through our senses: sight, smell, taste, touch and hearing. It is the combination of these, along with complex emotional factors, that create the "in love" experience. Feelings of love which have attracted you and your mate to one another help you begin bonding before marriage. An intimate sexual relationship within your marriage will fan the flames of your feelings and nourish your relationship. But sometimes problems occur when couples engage in sexual intercourse before marriage. Why? Stimulating the senses this way can heighten emotional feelings. In time, there is a failure to see that friendship-love and commitment-love hold marriages together when feelings change. Misused, the fire that warms and comforts the marriage can also burn and wound it beyond repair.[54] A fire brings warmth, light and the ability to cook and provide if properly contained in a fireplace. Light the fire in the middle of your living room floor and it will quickly spread and consume your whole house. Such is the same with pre-marital sex. Ministers would be wise to warn Christian couples of this and how waiting has great benefits. Sex is the beautiful gift God gives couples to open on their wedding night.

Friendship-love is the intimate and affectionate support of one another. Friendship-love is the heartbeat of a happy, healthy, and well functioning marriage. Within a marital relationship each spouse should be able to grow and develop. As each spouse grows, your relationship will be strengthened. Together, you create something new and become more than you can be alone. A friendship is a nurturing relationship born when two people receive love from one another, and it grows and becomes stronger as each person gives to the other. As you give to and share with your friend, the bond between the two of you is strengthened. You can value the love of a friend above all things. When your spouse is your friend and companion for life, your marriage will be a blessing to you both.

Friends possess a mutual trust allowing them to be vulnerable with one another. You trust friends with more than your secrets; you trust them with your very life. With your friends, you share your hopes, dreams, joys, and victories as well as your doubts, fears, sorrows, and failures. Your friends *accept* you fully. You possess a mutual concern for the well-being of the other. Value is the key word to describe the way you feel about your partner when you love them with Friendship-love. You care for what you value. *Where your treasure is, there your heart will be also.* – Matthew 6:21

Commitment-love is a pledge binding you to another for the rest of your life. Love that is faithful and permanent; that is Commitment-love. When you marry, you vow to love your spouse as God loves you. You tell your mate, "I am here, I will always be here, faithful and permanent, you can count on me." To be in a covenant relationship, you must accept that you are no longer your own. You belong to someone and someone belongs to you.[55]

For a successful marriage, you must first enter into a covenant or binding mutual agreement with someone greater than yourself. This is why God has covenanted with His people and the reason why you have God as your witness at your wedding ceremony. If you receive His Son Jesus Christ as your personal Lord and Savior, you are saved and your salvation is assured. When God covenants with us, He does not lose His identity. It is us who gains a sense of belonging to Him and His family. The same is true of marriage, we need a sense of belonging, but not to the point of losing ourselves. In Commitment-love, you allow the other person to grow and become all God has created them to be. This is the liberty of a committed marriage. In a marriage relationship, we must always balance our need for togetherness with our need to retain our own uniqueness. This type of Commitment-love leaves no room for words such as divorce or phrases such as, "I don't love you anymore." When you love unconditionally, you promise to give even if you do not receive. As a couple, you serve the institution of marriage and hold it in high esteem.

Other than giving your life to Christ, choosing to spend the rest of your life with someone is the most important decision you will ever make. You need to enter this covenant freely and willingly. If you feel trapped or coerced into making this commitment, resentment will build and your commitment will be difficult to keep. Commitment-love will make a marriage last, Friendship-love will make it strong, and Emotional-love will make it sweet.[56]

Wedding Guidelines Prior to Ceremony

- ❑ Since a wedding involves many individuals, the church should provide a wholesome atmosphere and a complete program of education in which young people may rightly mature in the matters of dating, becoming engaged, and planning for establishing a Christian home.
- ❑ Prior to the wedding, it would be helpful if the minister counseled the couple concerning such matters as: their spirituality, the basic responsibility of commitment and a maturing relationship, vocation and home finances, mutual fulfillment in the sexual relationship, planning for

children and the balance of home and church.
- ❏ The planning of the wedding, whether it be formal or informal, time and place and procedures for the rehearsal and wedding ceremony should be agreed upon as well.
- ❏ Laws governing marriage and divorce are under the authority of the state and vary from state to state. The minister should be familiar with the laws of their state. A proper marriage license is required, usually administered by local or county government. It will make life easier - *and the marriage legal!* - if you make it quite clear that you absolutely will not marry anyone unless they have the license in their hands *prior* to the wedding ceremony. You can require them to bring it to the rehearsal, usually the night before the ceremony. The marriage license should be obtained at the proper office governing the city where the ceremony is to be performed. Immediately AFTER the ceremony, *never* before the ceremony, you as the minister are to fill out and sign the license and put it in the mail. This is not the responsibility of the couple. Most states require a minister to be ordained before they can perform a wedding.
- ❏ Appropriate music should be chosen. Ordinary popular music should be avoided at a Christian wedding, but the minister should still marry the couple regardless of the music. As ministers, we represent Christ and must operate our lives in love.
- ❏ Etiquette is important within the wedding ceremony. The minister should dress in keeping

with that of the wedding party. Always ask the couple what they would like you to wear. Most of the time it is an ordinary street suit, but some times with a formal wedding, the couple may want you to be in a clerical robe.

- ❏ Electronic Devices. The minister should never ask to be in the wedding pictures, wait to be invited. While you may instruct the photographers on what you want them to do and especially *not do*, you are not paying them.
- ❏ Discuss your photography rules with the couple well before the ceremony so that they can instruct photographers. Videographers should not intrude on the wedding, nor should the placement of their equipments, especially lights. Prior to the ceremony, make an announcement reminding people to silence their phones. Airplane mode is safest as it makes no sound or vibration, but allows photos to be taken. Also, many people now stream their ceremonies online so absent friends and family can witness the live ceremony. Make sure this is done properly and without intruding on the ceremony. (People often forget to mute the device capturing the ceremony, thereby making it possible to hear the person watching.)

Personal Note: I do not perform weddings for couples without premarital counseling. I require a minimum of six 1½ hour sessions prior to the ceremony. The minister should also recommend several good books on marriage to the couple, such as:

— *One Flesh* by Bob Yandian

— *Sacred Influence* by Gary Thomas

— *The Purpose and Power of Love and Marriage* by Myles Munroe

— *Getting Ready For Marriage Workbook* by Jerry D. Hardin and Dianne Sloan

— *Called Together* by Steve and Mary Prokopchak

— *The Homebuilders Video Series* by Dennis Rainey

— *The Premarital Counseling Handbook* by H. Norman Wright

— *Christian Marital Counseling: Eight Approaches To Helping Couples* by Everett L. Worthington, Jr.

Pre-Marital Counseling Journal

An effective journal template assists in the organization and effectiveness of your counseling. Consider using this template of inquiries:

Counselor (Name):

Type of Counseling:

☐ Pre-marital ☐ Marriage ☐ General

Counseling Date #1

Counseling Date #2

Counseling Date #3

Counseling Date #4
Counseling Date #5
Counseling Date #6
Man (Name):
Woman (Name):
Are both people saved, yes or no? (1 Corinthians 7:39)
Man: ☐ Yes ☐ No
Woman: ☐ Yes ☐ No
Did you ask God for this mate, yes or no?
(Genesis 2:18)
Man: ☐ Yes ☐ No
Woman: ☐ Yes ☐ No
Are you members of a church?
Man: ☐ Yes ☐ No
Woman: ☐ Yes ☐ No
Will the wedding ceremony be in this church? If not, then where? Location? ☐ Sanctuary ☐ Chapel ☐ Fellowship Hall
Date and time of ceremony:
Agreed minimum: Six private sessions? ☐ Yes ☐ No
Is this a 1st, 2nd, 3rd marriage?
Man:
Woman:
What type of wedding do they want? ☐ Traditional ☐ Contemporary ☐ Other
Do you want the Minister to develop the vows and ceremony? ☐ Yes ☐ No
Are you willing to attend a wedding rehearsal?
☐ Yes ☐ No

Counseling Question #1 (2 Corinthians 6:14)
Do you both share a common life purpose?
Man: ☐ Yes ☐ No   Woman: ☐ Yes ☐ No

Marriage is God's primary tool for teaching us unselfishness, sensitivity, sacrifice, and mature love. To be married for 20, 30 or more years is a long time to live with someone. A poor understanding of each other will lead to a misunderstanding and conflict. You need to share something deeper. You need a common life purpose and that purpose must be God-centered. Two things can happen in a marriage. You can grow together, or you can grow apart, and 50% of married people are growing apart. To make a marriage work, you need to know what you want out of life and marry someone who wants the same thing.

Counseling Question #2 (Amos 3:3)
Do I feel safe expressing my feelings and thoughts with this person?
Man: ☐ Yes ☐ No   Woman: ☐ Yes ☐ No

This question goes right to the core of the quality of your relationship. Feeling safe means you can communicate openly with this person. This is the basis for establishing emotional intimacy. Its foundation is good communication and trust - i.e. trust so deep and strong that each person can state with confidence that, "I will not get punished or hurt for expressing my honest thoughts and feelings."

The opposite of this is exhibited by an abusive person, someone with whom you feel afraid to express your thoughts and feelings. A marriage with someone who does not allow you to express yourself safely and freely may last, but it will be rife with misery.

Counseling Question #3
Is he/she someone who is a sensitive person?
Man: ☐ Yes ☐ No   Woman: ☐ Yes ☐ No

Two people with Jesus Christ as their Savior leading them can go through anything, and have a greater potential than those without Christ. An imbalance or absence of this truth will cause difficulty in the marriage.

Are they attending church regularly?
Man: ☐ Yes ☐ No
Woman: ☐ Yes ☐ No
Are they tithing?
Man: ☐ Yes ☐ No
Woman: ☐ Yes ☐ No
Do they read the Bible often?
Man: ☐ Yes ☐ No
Woman: ☐ Yes ☐ No
Do they work on personal growth on a regular basis?
Man: ☐ Yes ☐ No
Woman: ☐ Yes ☐ No
Are they serious about improving themselves?
Man: ☐ Yes ☐ No
Woman: ☐ Yes ☐ No
What do they do with their time?
Man:
Woman:
Is this person materialistic?
Man: ☐ Yes ☐ No
Woman: ☐ Yes ☐ No

Usually a materialistic person is not someone whose top priority is character refinement through faith. There are essentially two types of people in the world: People who are dedicated to personal growth and people who are dedicated to seeking comfort. Someone whose goal in life is to be comfortable will put him or herself ahead of doing the right thing and doing for others, even for those they claim to love.

<u>Counseling Question #4</u>
How does he/she treat other people?

The ability to give constitutes the one most important thing that makes any relationship work. By giving, we mean the ability to provide another person with something meaningful to them, something healthy that pleases them, with nothing and no expectations in return. Is this someone who enjoys giving pleasure to others or are they wrapped up in themselves, vain and self-absorbed?

How do they treat strangers, such as waiters, busboys, taxi drivers, etc.? How do they treat their parents, step-parents, children, siblings, and neighbors? Do they have gratitude, appreciation and understanding of what God has given them, such as their salvation and provision? Do they gossip and speak badly about others? You can be sure that someone who treats others poorly will eventually treat <u>you</u> poorly as well.

<u>Counseling Question #5</u>
Is there anything I am hoping to change about this person after we're married?
Man: ☐ Yes ☐ No   Woman: ☐ Yes ☐ No

Too many people make the mistake of marrying someone with the intention of trying to improve them after they are married. You can probably expect someone to change after marriage, but it is usually not for the better. If you cannot fully accept and love this person the way they are now, do you think you will be able to later? Are you both observing the relationships around you, paying attention to their dynamics with honesty? Which relationships lift up and which ones lean over? Which ones encourage and which ones discourage? Which ones are on an upward path of growth and which ones are going downhill? When you leave certain people, or spend time with another couple, do you feel better or feel worse?

Objectively observing the relationships within your sphere gives keen insight into your own motivations for marriage. Are you being driven into marriage by: lust, desperation, loneliness, immaturity, ignorance, financial gain, pressure from others or a low self-esteem? If so, these can make you blind to all the warning signs.

Once you decide to commit to someone, their flaws, vulnerabilities, pet peeves, and differences become *more* obvious over time. If you love your mate and want the relationship to grow, you must learn to accept and embrace their flaws and not allow every little thing to bother you. You and your mate have many different expectations, emotional needs, values, dreams, weaknesses, and strengths. You are two unique, individual children of God who have decided to share a life together. Neither of you are perfect. Do you bring out the best in each other? Do you compliment and compromise with each other, or do you compete, compare, and control? Are you each other's advocates or adversaries? What are you willing to bring to the relationship? Have you come to give or to take? *Christians are supposed to be givers.*

Do you bring past relationships, past hurts, past mistrust, past wounds and biases into this marriage? *You cannot alter someone at the altar.* You cannot make someone love you or make someone stay. The work must be done beforehand. If you develop self-esteem, spiritual discernment, and a healthy, loving Christ-centered life, you will not find yourself making someone else responsible for your happiness or your pain. God is your happiness, not your spouse. Your spouse adds to your happiness.

Manipulation, control, jealousy, neediness, and selfishness are not the ingredients of a thriving, healthy, loving, and lasting relationship. Seeking status, sex, and security are also the wrong reasons to get married. More marriages die from inflexibility than from adultery, alcoholism, or abuse. If any of the following qualities are missing, the relationship will erode as resentment, withdrawal, abuse, neglect, dishonesty, and pain replace the passion.

To keep your relationship strong you need:
- ❏ Trust in God
- ❏ Communication
- ❏ Intimacy
- ❏ A sense of humor
- ❏ Sharing tasks
- ❏ Some getaway time without business, phone, or children
- ❏ Daily exchanges (a meal, shared activity, a hug,

a call, a touch, a note, an email or text)
- ❏ Sharing common purpose and interests
- ❏ Giving each other room to grow without feeling insecure
- ❏ Giving each other a sense of belonging and assurances of commitment

Six Characteristics of a Satisfying Marriage from Rick Warren

1. **Communication** – This is a skill you must learn through practice, but the bottom line is you've got to talk to each other. The average couple only spends four minutes a day talking to each other.
2. **Consideration** – The Bible teaches that we should show our love by being helpful to each other. Being considerate simply means paying attention to what your spouse says, showing common courtesy, and treating each other with respect.
3. **Compromise** – We're taught in the Bible that *"love does not demand its own way"* (1 Corinthians 13:5, TLB). The unloving thing to do is try to change your mate. Instead, you should yield your rights and learn the art of negotiation and compromise. Be flexible.
4. **Courtship** – If there was more courting in marriage, there'd be fewer marriages in court. You need to date your mate, making your relationship a priority, specifically developing things you like to do together.
5. **Commitment** – I find it interesting that the media has finally discovered the value of commitment.

Some headlines include: "Measuring our quality of life – happily married;" "Strong commitment brings satisfaction;" "Commitment is the key to marriage." There were many times in the first few years of our marriage when Kay or I might have bailed out, but we'd locked the escape hatch, agreeing that divorce was not an option. This forced us to change, to become flexible, to learn compromise, and to grow out of our selfishness.

6. **Christ** – Jesus gives you the power and the desire to develop the other five characteristics. He gives you love when you run out of love. The greatest thing you can do for your spouse is to become like Christ and then begin to treat your spouse like Christ would. *Marriage and Divorce* magazine discovered that one out of every three marriages ends in divorce, but when the couple is married in a church ceremony, and they attend church regularly, and they pray and read the Bible together, then the chances for divorce drop drastically. When both of you love Christ even more than you love each other, then you'll automatically grow together: Christ is not going to fight with Christ. As a word of testimony, nothing has challenged me so much as the challenge to build my marriage; yet nothing else in my life has been so rewarding. It is well worth the effort.

How Fear Damages a Marriage from Rick Warren

If we want our people to experience satisfying, intimate, and harmonious relationships with their mates, we must help them understand the importance of conquering fear. Successful marriages are built on trust and unconditional love, two things that can't exist alongside fear.

Fear damages marriage because it makes us:

Defensive – We hate to admit our weaknesses or mistakes. The fear that our spouse might see our faults and use them against us causes us to become defensive. Defensiveness causes two common reactions: we *accuse* our mates and we *excuse* ourselves. "It can't be me. It must be you." But that doesn't free you from your faults, and it doesn't help your marriage. In order to rid yourself of your faults, you must face them head on.

Distant – Men withdraw when faced with emotions. They become cool, detached, macho and cowardly. Women cry or get excited or angry, which makes men detach, which causes women to get more emotional. Rather than running, you need to talk about your feelings of anger or hurt.

Demanding – Insecurity demands that I must always be in control, must always have the last word, and must always have my way. Insecurity leads to power struggles. To prove his competence, the husband acts like a dictator; to prove her competence, the wife rebels. The result is that they live in a perpetual state of conflict. God doesn't mean for it to be that way.

The antidote to all this fear is transparency. The

most successful marriages are those based on total honesty.

Be honest with yourself. Face up to your faults, feelings and fears. Until you admit those things to yourself, you can't make any progress in your marriage.

Be honest to God. He already knows your faults; He's just waiting for you to admit them. He wants to help you, and He promises to love you no matter what.

Be honest with your mate. Admit your faults, feelings and fears. Start telling the truth to each other. Care enough to reveal yourself. There's simply no other way to develop intimacy than through the sharing of your faults, feelings, and fears. The greatest risk you'll ever take in your marriage is the risk of transparency, but it's also the most rewarding thing you can do.

Get rid of your fears and start enjoying a satisfying, successful marriage.

Relationship Wisdom:
- You go to each other for advice, and you almost always come away feeling better about things.
- You are supportive of each other's decisions, even when you just don't agree with them.
- You tell your honey when he or she has hurt you, instead of holding a grudge.
- You are generally able to resolve fights to your mutual satisfaction.
- You both know that relationships take work, and you are willing to go the distance.
- You respect, admire, listen to, and just plain like each other.
- You share enough of the same interests and friends

so you don't feel like you're on your own.
• You have similar spending/saving habits, or you've discussed how you'll each compromise to keep the peace.
• You have the same attitude about paying bills or debt management.
• You are aware of each other's total present debt, if any.
• You have discussed how you will merge your finances once you get married and you are comfortable with the plan.
• You have told your honey about all your money and have no hidden nest eggs, "just in case."
• You have similar definitions of a comfortable income, and similar or symbiotic income goals.

Sex
• Your sexual needs are compatible, and you are both satisfied.
• You are comfortable giving and taking sexual suggestions and requests.
• Birth control is something you consider a joint responsibility, and you have openly discussed your options and preferences.
• You use sex as a healthy and fun expression of your love, not as a way to gloss over problematic issues in your relationship, a weapon, or an easy way to solve disputes (without addressing the root of the argument).
• You don't use sex, or the denial of sex to manipulate or punish. Sex is an expression of love and must not be tampered with.
• You have confessed your sexual past and had frank discussions about STDs and previous partners.

Family

• You generally get along with each other's families (general friendliness and goodwill), and if not, you've at least discussed to what extent they will play a role in your future family life.

• You are willing and prepared to regard each other as your most important familial relationship after you get married.

• You have similar faith and have discussed how to incorporate church into your future family.

• You have talked about children - how many you want, or if you want them at all.

• If you have children from a previous marriage, your mate treats them with respect and kindness.

• You have considered not only the future responsibility of caring for your spouse, but also the possibility of caring for their parents or other family members.[57]

The Wedding Rehearsal

The rehearsal is the place that the wedding participants, including the bride and groom, family, singers, musicians, and ushers as well as the wedding party learn and practice their responsibilities and timing for the ceremony. Tradition has it that it is the bride's prerogative to plan the wedding. The minister should go over all the plans and wishes thoroughly before the wedding rehearsal. At the rehearsal, the minister will tactfully carry out the bride's plans, though as the officiant they will offer advice where needed. The minister is in charge of keeping order at the rehearsal, and more importantly at the ceremony.

The wedding rehearsal is usually held on the evening of the day before the wedding. Plans should be agreed upon ahead of time, especially the time for the rehearsal. As a minister, you will save yourself much grief if you instruct the couple that the only people allowed at the rehearsal are the people in the wedding party. The wedding rehearsal should be approximately 30 to 60 minutes in length. At the author's first wedding he performed, 130 people showed up for the rehearsal. The wedding party and most of the guests and family. It was pandemonium lasting almost 3 hours.

Take the ushers aside and make certain they know how to properly seat the guests. Most have never had to do anything like this before. Have them practice so that the wedding day is not their first time. The processional may vary somewhat, due to the number of attendants, arrangement of the church aisles and plans of the couple. Generally at a prearranged signal (with music or the wedding planner) the minister, groom, best man, and groomsmen will make their appearance, in that order, coming in from a side door and take their places at the altar. The bride enters from another door, traditionally symbolic of the bride and groom coming from two different walks of life and meeting together before God. The minister will stand in the center and the men at his left, facing the guests. Be aware that sometimes the bride will want the ushers to walk down the aisle with the bridesmaids and take their places at the front. Discuss this in advance.

Next will come the maid of honor, bridesmaids, ring bearer and flower girls and last, the bride on the left arm of her father, designee, or alone if preferred. The bridesmaids will take their place at the altar to the right of the minister with the maid of honor at the minister's side. The bride and her father or designee stand directly in front of the minister. In most areas, it is customary for the guests to rise at the appearance of the bride, or they may stand at the appearance of the minister. When the bride reaches the altar, the minister will indicate that the guests may be seated.

The order of the recessional is the reverse of the processional. The minister may either walk out with the wedding party as they retire, or remains standing at the altar until they exit, after which he retires to the door he entered. Discuss this in advance.

Some final instructions for the wedding party at the rehearsal:

1. The wedding party should arrive 60 minutes prior

to the time of the ceremony.
2. The groom's mother is to be seated by an usher in the first pew at the right facing the chancel, pulpit or lectern.
3. The head usher will seat the bride's mother in the first pew to the left of the pulpit.
4. If candles will be used, they should be lit 15 minutes before the ceremony.
5. If unity candle or colored sand (blended families) are to be used, they should be properly placed. Groom brings these.
6. If the couple wants to partake of Communion at the ceremony, the minister is to make sure that the communion table is in full view of the guests. Decide ahead of time who will bring the bread and the wine. Usually, just the minister and the couple partake of the elements.
7. Be careful about letting little children carry the rings. The best man usually takes both rings from the ring bearer and holds them for the minister.
8. Last, but not least, the minister cannot marry them without the license. The author likes to have the license in hand at the rehearsal.

On the day of the wedding, the minister must arrive at least 60 minutes prior to the start of the ceremony. The author has performed numerous wedding ceremonies, and in doing so has found the couple always wants to make some last minute changes. Above all, the minister must be fluid. Suggest to the bride that the florist arrive two hours in advance of the ceremony to do final decorating.

The minister's poise is the key to a well

regulated wedding ceremony. He or she should be so familiar with all the particulars of the ceremony, that one can impart calmness and inspire confidence. Remember, once the music starts, the minister is in charge. You must show that you are in full command of the situation. Should a mistake occur (and they always do), remind the couple that scarcely anyone will notice. The minister must not become confused during the ceremony, but must give calm instruction and prompting, just as though this is what the ceremony called for. [58] The author usually prints out the wedding liturgy and has it taped into a colored folder to read at the ceremony. I do not ever stand behind a podium, but rather position myself right before the couple in plain view of the guests. I also have the couple face each other, so the guests can see their faces, not their backs through the ceremony.

Wedding Ceremony Positions

Pulpit/Chancel

†

Minister

Flower Girl · · · · · · · · · · · · · · · Ring Bearer

Maid of Honor · · · **Bride** · · · **Groom** · · · Best Man

BM BM BM BM BM · · · · · · · · · · · GM GM GM GM GM

Bride's Parents · **Groom's Parents**
  (Grand) Mother Father BM GM (Grand) Mother Father

Bride's Special Guests/Children BM GM Groom's Special Guests/Children

Bride's Guests · · · · · · BM GM · · · · · · Groom's Guests
 · · · · · · · · · · · · · · · BM
 · · · · · · · · · · · · · · · BM
 · · · · · · · · · · · · · · · BM

Bride's side of Church ↑ **Groom's side of Church**

Usher · · · · · · Usher · · · · · · Usher

Formal Wedding Liturgy

1. Musical Prelude
2. Processional
3. Prayer of Invocation (Invoking the Spirit of God)
4. Call to Worship (Announcement of the purpose of the service)
5. Special Selected Music
6. Scripture Reading (Ex. 1 John 4:16-19)
7. Wedding Address (optional) poems, message from another family member
8. Declaration of Intent (Couple being married on Christian terms)
9. Wedding Homily (short sermon)
10. Giving Away of the Bride (traditionally to approach altar here) Bride, Groom, Maid of Honor and Best Man
11. Prayer of Blessing (Over the couple)
12. Exchange of Vows
13. Exchange of Rings
14. Lighting of the Unity Candles (optional - couple alone or with children)
15. Pronouncement of Marriage (Minister to couple & congregation, "I now pronounce you husband & wife.")
16. Communion (optional)
17. The Lord's Prayer (optional)
18. Benediction
19. Introduction of the Couple
20. Recessional

Formal Wedding Ceremony

1. Musical Prelude
2. Processional - The Entrance (Everyone to stand)
3. Prayer of Invocation (Congregation asked to be seated, Bride and Groom facing minister)
4. Call to Worship - Announcement of Purpose of Service

Minister to All: Dear Family and Friends, we are assembled here today in the presence of God to unite (groom's name_____) and (bride's name_____) in holy matrimony. The Bible teaches that marriage is instituted by God, and to be held in honor among all men. It is to be a permanent relationship of one man and one woman freely and totally committed to each other as companions for life. Our Lord declared that a man shall leave his father and mother and unite with his wife and the two shall become one flesh. Let us therefore reverently remember that God has established and sanctified marriage for the welfare and happiness of all mankind.

5. Special Selected Music
6. Scripture Reading (1 John 4:16-19) And so we know and rely on the love God has for us. God is love. Whoever lives in love lives in God, and God in him. In this way, love is made complete among us so that we will have confidence on the Day of Judgment, because in this world we are like him. There is no fear in love. But perfect love drives out fear, because fear has to do with punishment. The one who fears is not made

perfect in love. We love because he first loved us.

7. Wedding Address (optional - acknowledging the children, a poem, or special song or item expressed)

8. Declaration of Intent (Couple being married on Christian terms, then right into the homily)

Minister to All: The home is built upon love, and this virtue is best portrayed in the 13th chapter of Paul's first letter to the Corinthians. Love is patient, love is kind. It does not envy, it does not boast, it is not proud. It is not rude, it is not self-seeking, it is not easily angered, it keeps no record of wrongs. Love does not delight in evil but rejoices with the truth. It always protects, always trusts, always hopes, always perseveres. Love never fails.

Marriage is a companionship which involves mutual commitment and mutual responsibility. You share alike in the responsibilities and the joys of life. When companions share a sorrow, the sorrow is halved, and when they share a joy, the joy is doubled. You are exhorted to dedicate your home to your Creator and take His Word the Bible for your marriage guide. Give loyal devotion to His church, thus uniting the mutual strength of these two most important institutions, the marriage and God's church, living your lives as His willing servants, and true happiness will be your temporal and eternal reward. Amen.

9. Giving Away of the Bride

Who gives the bride to be married? Bride's father: I DO or he may say HER MOTHER and I do.

Who presents this man & woman to be married? Both families: WE DO

10. Prayer of Blessing

Minister: Let us pray. Oh Lord of life and love, bestow your grace upon this marriage and seal this commitment of your children with your love. As you have brought them together by your divine providence, sanctify them by your Holy Spirit that they may give themselves fully to one another and to you. Give them strength and patience to live in a manner that will mutually bless them in honor of your holy name through Jesus Christ our Lord, Amen.

11. Exchange of Vows (couple facing each other holding both hands, flowers to flower girl)

Minister to Groom: - (First & Last Name_____) will you take (First & Last Name_____) to be your wife? Will you commit yourself to her happiness and her self-fulfillment as a person, and to her usefulness in God's Kingdom; and will you promise to love, honor, trust, and serve her in sickness and in health, in adversity and prosperity and be true and loyal to her so long as you both shall live? ***Groom***: I WILL

Minister to Bride: - (First & Last Name_____) will you take (First & Last Name_____) to be your husband? Will you commit yourself to his happiness and his self-fulfillment as a person, and to his usefulness in God's Kingdom; and will you promise to love, honor, trust and serve him in sickness and in health, in adversity and prosperity and be true and loyal to him so long as you both shall live? ***Bride***: I WILL

12. Scripture: Hebrews 13:4 Marriage should be honored by all, and the marriage bed kept pure, for God will judge the adulterer. **Exchange of Rings** (Ring bearer gives rings to Minister, couple still facing each other)

Minister to All: (Holding up a ring) The wedding ring is a symbol of marriage in at least two ways: The purity of gold symbolizes the love of Christ for His children and your love for each other. The unending circle symbolizes Christ's unending love and covenant with us, as well as the vows you are making to each other. These vows which you are taking may only be broken honorably in the sight of God by death. As a token of your vows you will give and receive the rings.

Minister to Groom: (Repeat after Me) (with pauses)
With this ring, I (First & Last Name_____) take you (First & Last Name_____), to be my wedded wife, to have and to hold, from this day forward, for better or for worse, for richer or for poorer, in sickness and in health, to love and to cherish, till death do us part. I hereby pledge to you my faithfulness, in the name of the Father and of the Son and of the Holy Spirit.

Minister to Bride: (Repeat after Me) (with pauses)
With this ring, I (First & Last Name_____), take you (First & Last Name_____), to be my wedded husband, to have and to hold, from this day forward, for better or for worse, for richer or for poorer, in sickness and in health, to love and to cherish, till death do us part. I hereby pledge to you my faithfulness, in the name of the Father and of the Son and of the Holy Spirit.

13. Lighting of the Unity Candles or Colored Sand (optional)

Minister to Couple: (First Name) and (First Name), the two lighted candles symbolize your separate lives, your separate families and your separate sets of friends before today. I ask that you each light one candle and that together you light the center candle. (Pause for lighting) The individual candles represent your individual lives before today. Lighting the center candle represents that your two lives are now joined to one Light, and that Light is Jesus Christ. He is the Light of the world, and whoever follows Him shall never walk in darkness. The center candle also represents the joining together of your two families and two sets of friends to become one.

14. Pronouncement of Marriage (couple facing Minister)
Minister to Congregation and the Couple: Since they have made these commitments before the eyes of God and this assembly, what God has joined together, let no man separate. In as much as the two of you have agreed to live together in Holy Matrimony, you have promised your love for each other by these vows, the giving of these rings and the joining of your hands, **by the authority vested in me by Almighty God and the laws of this State, I now pronounce you husband and wife.**

(Husband's first name), you may now kiss your bride.

15. Communion / The Lord's Prayer or Both (Minister and the couple only for communion)

Minister to All: Because a wedding ceremony is a worship service, (husband's name) and (wife's name) have decided to incorporate Communion into their wedding ceremony, making Communion their very first act of worship as a married couple.

16. Benediction (Numbers 6:24-26)
Minister to All: May the Lord bless you and keep you. May the Lord make his face shine upon you, and be gracious unto you. May the Lord lift up his countenance unto you, and give you peace.

17. Introduction of the Couple
Minister to All: It gives me great pleasure to introduce to you for the first time, Mr. & Mrs._____.

Other Great Wedding Scriptures Are:
Genesis 2:18, 22-24, Proverbs 31:10-12, Romans 15:5-7, Ephesians 4:32, 5:1-2, 22-28, 1 Corinthians 13:4-8a, Philippians 2:2-3, Colossians 3:13-15, 1 Peter 4:8-10.

Suggested Post Ceremony Receiving Line Order:
Mother of Bride, Mother of Groom, Father of Groom, Father of Bride, Bride, Groom, Maid of Honor, Bridesmaids, Best Man, Groomsmen.

Informal Wedding Ceremony

The contemporary or informal wedding may take place in the couple's home, or in the home of the minister, in a chapel, a park, etc. The couple may wish to be accompanied by their parents only and a few selected friends. This type of ceremony is usually more brief than the formal ceremony. It includes all of the essentials, yet sometimes the couple prefers to write their own vows.

As a minister, be very careful. Review their vows, you do not want to compromise the Word of God, simply because the ceremony is less formal or not taking place in a church. The author does not marry anyone who wishes to omit the name of Jesus from the ceremony. Also, there may not be any rehearsal, but just an informal meeting about who does what, 30 minutes prior to the service. Whether a contemporary or home wedding, the minister may use the formal liturgy and make certain necessary adjustments. There may or may not be a processional or recessional. The minister may offer a quick benediction (blessing) over the couple. Family members and friends may then gather around the couple to offer their congratulations.[59]

Informal Wedding Liturgy:

1. Musical Prelude
2. Prayer of Invocation (invoking the Spirit of God)
3. Call to Worship (announcement of the purpose of the service)
4. Scripture Reading (Example - 1 John 4:16-19)
5. Wedding Address (optional) poems, message from another family member
6. Wedding Homily (short sermon)
7. Exchange of Vows
8. Exchange of Rings
9. Lighting of the Unity Candles (optional)
10. Pronouncement of Marriage (Minister to couple & congregation, "I now pronounce you husband & wife.")
11. Benediction (blessing)
12. Introduction of the Couple (optional)

Renewal of Vows

A service for renewal of vows may be requested by married couples at wedding anniversaries or upon other significant occasions. This is particularly fitting for the golden wedding anniversary conducted in the home, or at the 10, 20 or 30 year milestones. A renewal of vows service may also be conducted at a regular Sunday worship service where some married couples renew their vows as an emphasis upon the Christian home and their devotion to Christ. The minister may read an appropriate passage of Scripture, emphasizing the importance of the home.[60]

A renewal of wedding vows ceremony can be a meaningful and touching ceremony for the couple, their children, family, and friends. As a married couple, it is a time to pause and reflect on where the couple has been and where they are going. It is also a wonderful example to set for their children and grandchildren. Just imagine the beautiful scene of children watching their parents joining hands and hearts as they affirm the magnitude and strength of their enduring love. What greater life/love lesson? It is often said at these ceremonies: "True love does not wither or die. It merely ripens."

Vow renewal ceremonies can be as creative and personal as the couple wants them to be. **Here are some things you can suggest to the re-new couple:**

- ❏ Walk down the aisle to classical music and walk out to "your song."

- ❏ Let the cover of your invitation feature your grandchild's favorite drawing of Grandma and Pop or even your first wedding portrait.
- ❏ Play your original wedding video at your reception or display original picture.
- ❏ Buy new wedding bands for the occasion and have them specially engraved.
- ❏ The ceremony can be conducted in churches, chapels, temples, banquet facilities, on yachts, out of doors or in the privacy of a couple's home – with a room full of guests or in an intimate setting with just the couple. The couples themselves host the celebration because it is so very personal. It is a decision that only you as a couple can make.
- ❏ Your ceremony should be less formal than a wedding, more casual and fun.
- ❏ When writing your own personalized wedding vows, jot down words or phrases you both like. Look to answer the question: How do I love my husband/wife now? Have they made me a better person? What am I most grateful for to my husband/wife?

Some couples choose to renew their vows after a particularly difficult crisis in their lives, say for example, the overcoming of a serious illness or a period of estrangement. Others simply want to reaffirm the tremendous love that has matured and deepened with the passing of years.

Vow renewals are usually conducted by clergy since they are generally more spiritual and not official in nature. *Unlike weddings, no legal paperwork is needed for a vow renewal.*

A minister may state the following "Declaration of Intent" before the couple takes the standard wedding vows:

"When you first joined hands and hearts ___ years ago, you did not know where life would take you. You promised to love, honor and cherish one another through all things. Life has surely brought you both wonderful blessings and difficult tribulations. Therefore, you have fulfilled your promise and God is smiling! So, as you come here today to reaffirm your wedding vows and as you reflect back over all the years as husband and wife, do you now reaffirm the vows you took ___ years ago? If so, repeat after me (personal vows here)." [61]

Another sample vow idea might be: "You are mine, my love, and I am yours, as ordained by God from the beginning of time. God brought us together, kept us together. You are God's gift to me, my priceless treasure, my blessing for life. May God bless us as we come together before our family and friends to renew our pledge of love to one another, eternal."

Other Vow Renewal Ceremony Guidelines:
- ❑ Involve the children.
- ❑ It is customary for the husband to escort the wife down the aisle.
- ❑ Maybe recreate your original wedding cake.
- ❑ Return to your original honeymoon destination.
- ❑ Display your first wedding photograph.
- ❑ Display photographs of your first wedding guests.[62]

Wedding Vow Renewal Samples:

"Once before, I have stood with you before family and friends, once again, I take your hand as my partner. (Name), I take you this day, and for all days, as my (husband/wife)."

"I am proud to marry you on this day. I promise to wipe away your tears with my laughter and your pain with my caring and compassion. We will wipe clean the old canvases of our lives and let God, with His amazing artistic talent, fill them with new colors, harmony and beauty. I give myself to you completely, and I promise to love you always, from this day forth."

"I believe in this marriage more strongly than ever. (Name), it is with joy born of experience and trust that I commit myself once again to be your (husband/wife)."

"I, (name), give to you, (name), a new promise, and yet not so new; a new (husband/wife), and yet not so new; and a new affirmation of love from the heart that has loved you for ( ) years and will love you for as many more as God allows." [63]

Funerals

Funeral Principles

No demands upon a minister or Christian leader are greater than the call to minister in the hour of bereavement and death. Never do people need you more or lean upon you as heavily as now, when death has overtaken the life of someone they love. It is your responsibility to show them that Jesus grieves with them. Deep, traumatic grief opens wide the door to Jesus, inviting His lost and hurting children into His love and mercy. As a minister, you are to demonstrate how the Savior arrives to comfort them in their loss.[64]

Bereavement is so much more than just a difficult time. It is confusing, stressful, exhausting, and sometimes sickening. The bereaved person will often feel that their experience is unique, that no one has ever endured such a loss or suffered as they are suffering.

Your job is to guide them through the pain and healing process and into a sense of renewal and hope. Knowing the cycle of grief, which permits the sorrowing person to recover in due time, will allow you to understand and explain the complexities of this difficult journey. Through this process, and grieving is a process, you are to help the bereaved discover a new reality. Yet, for some people, complete recovery may not come.

The cycle of healing from grief usually proceeds as follows:

1. The Initial Shock of Death - That intense emotional impact which sometimes leaves a person with a seeming paralysis. They may also become hyperactive in an attempt to quell the pain.
2. Emotional Release - A time characterized by weeping, anger, or extreme emotional outbursts. This is normal as long as it does not persist.
3. Loneliness and Depression - A sense of loss often related to the degree of dependence on the deceased. The person may feel they have lost a part of their own identity through the death of a loved one. Often, this is experienced as a loss of self.
4. Guilt - A feeling of guilt characterized by second guessing, "I could have done more" or "I should have said this, etc."
5. Anger and Hostility - "Why did God do this to me?"
6. Inertia or Listlessness - "I can't get on with life" or "I couldn't care less."
7. A Gradual Return to Hope - "Life will go on" or "I will be able to cope" or "God will get me over this."
8. The Return to Reality - Admitting the loss and adjusting to it.[65]

Helping grieving people calls for total authenticity, sensitivity, tenderness, and empathy. As a leader, you must depend on the Holy Spirit for guidance. Do not use glib or pat answers. Be sincere and meaningful in all you do and say. The kind of comfort you provide depends on where the person is in the grieving process. Do not pretend to have an answer for everything. Admit that you do not understand why or how God does what He does. You don't have all the answers. Don't pretend that you do. If fact, admit up front that you don't. Do not be a cheerleader trying to bring cheer and goodwill. Do not offer clichés or phrases about death and suffering or suggest that if the grieving person were more spiritual or closer to God, the pain might be less.

Remember as a minister, that one short pre-funeral family visit will not meet all the needs of the bereaved. The best way to share Jesus is to imitate Him. Then, do what you can to share Jesus Christ and the message of Scripture, and trust God to do His work.[66]

After the minister receives notification of death:
1. Immediately upon learning of the death, the minister should go with all due haste to the family, whether in the hospital or at home. A few quiet words, a Scripture verse, and a brief prayer are usually offered. If asked to conduct the funeral service, the minister will arrange to come later to assist in making the plans.
2. At the appointed time, the minister will go to the home to plan for the funeral service. The time for the funeral should be decided by the family, the funeral director, and the minister. Try to meet the request of the family for music and other items in the service, as long as they are in good taste and in keeping with the Christian content and order.
3. The primary purpose of the funeral service is to aid people in working through their grief, provide meaning for the deceased, and a chance to say goodbye to their loved one.

4. The funeral service should lead people to face the reality of death as well as the reality of life. The funeral home and the funeral director are indispensable at this time. They handle many of the details of the funeral such as: casket and vault purchase, wake, cemetery interment, headstone, etc. The prudent minister will collaborate with them.
5. In this service, the church has an opportunity through the minister to express its affirmation of Christian faith. Here the power of the resurrection and the meaning of Christian commitment should be set forth.
6. A brief funeral meditation is usually appropriate and its purpose should be to interpret, affirm truth, support and comfort the bereaved, and to provide a challenge for future living. The minister should neither condemn nor stress the faults and sins of the deceased. The truth of God's Word will provide the necessary intervention.
7. For some family members, viewing the body can be meaningful in accepting the reality of death, separation, and loss. This should always be done prior to the service. The casket could be open or closed at the wake, but should be closed at the funeral service to indicate the place of separation and to point to the spiritual and eternal value of knowing Christ.
8. If the family wants a eulogy (sermon at a funeral), the minister should formulate his or her eulogy around information gathered at the pre-funeral family meeting.

9. The funeral service provides a great opportunity for an invitation for people to receive Christ as their Lord and Savior. For some at the funeral service, this may be their first time hearing the Gospel. This must be done with great care, however. The focus must be on the deceased within the context of God's Kingdom.
10. The church and community should be encouraged to remember the bereaved in prayer and to help the family adjust to life.
11. There are many variations to the order of a funeral service appropriate to family needs and their particular situation.[67]

Guidelines for Performing a Funeral

1. Remember the deceased with appreciation and demonstrate love and support for the relatives.
2. Provide a means of healing through prayer and reaffirm eternal life with Scripture.
3. Make sure the people involved in the service are identified and know what to do.
4. Make sure everyone understands the funeral liturgy (order of service).
5. The minister should pay respects to the family before entering the pulpit.
6. Music should be religious, not secular. A funeral in a Christian church led by a Christian minister must worship Christ.

7. The Gospel should be clear during the eulogy. Our hope of heaven as believers should be evident.
8. Give an invitation to accept Christ at the end of the service.
9. Always expect interruptions, awkward moments and yes, mistakes, at funerals.
10. The minister should greet the family, relatives and friends as they exit the church.

Sample Funeral Service Liturgy:

1. Musical Prelude
2. Processional
3. Hymn
4. Old Testament Reading
5. New Testament Reading
6. Prayer
7. Special Music
8. Reading of the Resolution and the Obituary
9. Special Music
10. Eulogy
11. Recessional
12. At Graveside – Body Committal

The Funeral Service with Eulogy

Musical Prelude – Quiet organ music or soft recorded music played through the church's sound system should be heard while guests are being seated.

Processional – The senior pastor with associate ministers following and the family following them (unless the immediate family are already seated) make their way into the sanctuary. The senior pastor asks the congregation to stand. The pastor may recite Scripture out loud as the family makes their way down the church aisle.

Hymn – Special live music or solo.

Old Testament Reading – (Isaiah 43:1-3 NIV)
But now, this is what the Lord says, he who created you O' Jacob, he who formed you O' Israel: "Fear not, for I have redeemed you; I have summoned you by name; you are mine. When you pass through the waters, I will be with you; and when you pass through the rivers, they will not sweep over you. When you walk through the fire, you will not be burned, the flames will not set you ablaze. For I am the Lord your God, the Holy One of Israel, your Savior; . . ."

New Testament Reading – (Revelation 21:1-4 NIV)
Then I saw a new heaven and a new earth, for the first heaven and the first earth had passed away, and there was no longer any sea. I saw the Holy City, the New Jerusalem, coming down out of heaven from God, prepared as a bride beautifully dressed for her husband. And I heard a loud voice from the throne

saying, "Now the dwelling of God is with men, and he will live with them. They will be his people, and God himself will be with them and be their God. He will wipe every tear from their eyes. There will be no more death or mourning or crying or pain, for the old order of things has passed away."

Prayer – Father, Lord Jesus and Holy Spirit, we love you and praise you this day. Lord we ask you to bring comfort upon this family in their time of sorrow. Lord, we rejoice in the knowing that Jesus has paid the way that all of us who believe may enter heaven and be saved. Give this family comfort and direction and answers in their time of need. May everything that we think, say and do bring glory and honor to your precious name. Save, sanctify and set free in this service, and be glorified in the name of your Son Jesus Christ we pray, Amen.

Special Words – Family and friends are given two minutes each in the pulpit to give testimonies, read poems, or pay tribute to the deceased.

Reading of the Resolution (Words of comfort from the Senior Pastor. This can be read by any member of staff or a lay leader.) Here is a sample resolution - "We continue in faith, love and joy at a time when there is so much sorrow. Our flesh feels the pain, but our spirit is excited because we look forward to seeing (deceased name) again in glory. We are not here to mourn (deceased name), but rather, to celebrate her/his home-going. Be it resolved that we humbly submit ourselves to our Heavenly Father who does all things well. We lift up the family to Him for only He is able to console you at this difficult time. Rest in the knowledge that He will be with you to strengthen and support you as you go through these days of adjustment. Our Heavenly Father understands your pain and only He brings comfort, hope and joy in the midst of it. Be it resolved that our Senior Pastor, Officers and members of (Church Name) express our prayers, love and support to the entire family."

Reading of the Obituary – This can be read by the Pastor, a Christian leader of the church, staff member, family member or friend. The obituary has already been created by a member of the family and most likely posted on the internet or in a newspaper.

Special Music – Hymn or solo to invoke the Spirit of God over the preached Word about to come forth.

Eulogy – This is an example of a sermon at a funeral: Jesus Himself speaking in the Gospel of John 14:1-3 "Do not let your hearts be troubled. You believe in God; believe also in me.² My Father's house has many rooms; if that were not so, I would have told you. I am going there to prepare a place for you,³ and if I go and prepare a place for you, I will come back and take you to be with me, that you also may be where I am."

These final conversations that Jesus had with His disciples while He was here on earth have been preserved for us by John in chapters 14-17 of his Gospel. I would like to speak with you for a few minutes on *"A Home with Many Rooms"*.

Sometimes our most cherished sources of comfort are shattered in the presence of one inevitable fact of life, death comes to us all. The opening words of chapter 14 are particularly meaningful and reassuring, because here, Jesus talks about death as the journey home and about our life beyond death as life in our new home. The trip home may be easy or rough; it may be untimely or timed with divine grace.

For Christians, however, there can be no doubt about the destination. If you are a child of God by adoption through Jesus Christ, you may look forward to sharing His risen life with Him in the presence of His Father, who is also our Father. Beyond death, there is life – and this life is in the Father's house. The metaphor of heaven as God's home, where we hope to be with God for all eternity, is well-known.

At the beginning of John 14, however, Jesus says something that fleshes out the image in a way that is truly nourishing to faith and hope. "In my Father's house there are many rooms," says the Lord. What does this image suggest? This image suggests that heaven is spacious, comfortable and gracious. There is something poetically and theologically right about picturing heaven as God's home, designed by God with supreme artistry, sufficient for God and God's numberless family, and suffused with love, which all the members of the family share with God and with one another.

The image of the home with many rooms also symbolizes the diversity of God's people. Even within the 12 apostles, there were not just contrasts, but extremes – like Matthew, the tax collector for Rome, and Simon the Zealot, the armed rebel against Rome. And by the time John wrote his Gospel, the ranks of Christians had grown so greatly in both numbers and diversity that you had to picture that house with many rooms – just to keep them from arguing throughout eternity! The image of the home with many rooms also suggests reunion.

We need more than just God and strangers, even though they are our brothers and sisters in the faith. We need some of the people who made God real for us in this life, some of the people whose love made it possible for us to believe in a God of love. Not to see (deceased person's name) again or not to be reunited with our loved ones would NOT be heaven. It would be hell!

The image of a mansion or a home with many rooms is apt, not only because it projects a reunited family, but because it offers the members of the family some privacy. Each of us will have his or her own room, specially designed by God. It is touchingly beautiful that John has Jesus stake his truthfulness on this promise of heaven as our new home. Jesus was undeniably truthful with His disciples. Whoever was seeking a crown, Jesus would offer him a cross, just as He Himself would be wearing a crown of thorns. So if He was truthful about everything in this life, they could trust His promise of life beyond death, in the Father's house, where there would be many rooms.

But the most important and most comforting part of the promise still follows. "I go to prepare a place for you," says the Lord. "I will come again and will receive you unto myself, so that where I am, there you may be also." As a Minister, I base all of my life on God's Word and like all other mortal humans, I will one day die as well. But God's Word can be trusted. When God reclaims our life, His gift that He created, when we pass through death, we shall be with Jesus, our risen Lord for all eternity. And the Bible says that there will be no more pain, no more suffering, and God Himself will wipe away every tear and we will finally be home. (Deceased person's name) has crossed over and is in his/her room right now. And listen….. he/she has never been more alive…… all because of Jesus. This alone is incredibly priceless, Amen.

Invitation to Receive Christ (See Salvation Prayers earlier in the Handbook on page 47)

Recessional – The pastor pays final respects to the immediate family and proceeds out of the sanctuary ahead of the associate ministers, with the immediate family next. Then the funeral home staff with the casket. The funeral director escorts the family to the limo for the ride to the cemetery. Usually soft music is playing.

At the Cemetery

- ❑ The minister may choose to take his/her own car or ride with the funeral director.
- ❑ The minister leads the pallbearers ahead of the casket speaking the Word of God aloud as they approach the grave. Consider memorizing John 14:1-6 KJV for this procession.

Minister Reads While Walking: "Let not your heart be troubled: ye believe in God, believe also in me. In my Father's house are many mansions: if it were not so,

I would have told you. I go to prepare a place for you. And if I go and prepare a place for you, I will come again, and receive you unto myself; that where I am, there ye may be also. And whither I go ye know, and the way ye know. Thomas saith unto him, Lord, we know not whither thou goest; and how can we know the way? Jesus saith unto him, I am the way, the truth, and the life: no man cometh unto the Father, but by me."

The Minister then stands at the head of the casket waiting for family members and friends to gather for prayer. (Graveside service is 15 mins.)

Prayer at Graveside:

Minister: Let us pray. Heavenly Father, we acknowledge the reality of death as we stand here today. Although death separates loved ones, make us aware that it is only for a season. Although it brings grief, may we look to your Spirit to bring comfort and peace. Although death brings disappointment, give us faith to look to the future with hope and courage. Father, abide with these our friends throughout the coming days, and bring us all together again around your throne in eternal glory. This we pray in the name of Jesus Christ our Lord, Amen.

Scripture Reading at Graveside:

Minister: (1 Thessalonians 4:13-18) Brothers and sisters, we do not want you to be uninformed about those who sleep in death, so that you do not grieve like the rest of mankind, who have no hope. For we believe that Jesus died and rose again, and so we believe that God will bring with Jesus those who have fallen asleep in him. According to the Lord's word, we tell you that we who are still alive, who are left until the coming of the Lord, will certainly not precede those who have fallen asleep. For the Lord himself will come down from heaven, with a loud command, with the voice of the archangel and with the trumpet call of God, and the dead in Christ will rise first. After that, we who are still alive and are left will be caught up together with them in the clouds, to meet the Lord in the air. And so, we will be with the Lord forever. Therefore encourage one another with these words.

Body Committal: - *(Committing the body to God and into the final resting place)*

Minister: Merciful Father, remind us of the words of our Lord Jesus, "Blessed are those who mourn, for they will be comforted." Show us how to mourn our brother/sister *(full name)* freely and deeply, as disciples of the Master, who Himself felt no shame about weeping at the death of His friend Lazarus. But, remind us also of Jesus' power to restore us to life. Our hope is in Christ who loved us and gave His life for us. In the name of our Lord Jesus Christ, crucified and risen, we commend to God's merciful care our brother/sister *(full name)*, and we commit his/her body to their original elements: *(Repeat the following words while simultaneously placing 3 flowers on top of the casket, one at a time, given to the minister by the funeral director)* Earth to earth *(flower)*, ashes to ashes *(flower)*, dust to dust *(last flower)*. "Blessed are they who die in the Lord ... for they will rest from their labors and their works do follow them." In the name of the Father, and of the Son, and of the Holy Spirit, Amen.

Benediction

Minister: The Lord bless you and keep you. The Lord make His face shine upon you and be gracious unto you. The Lord lift up His countenance upon you, and give you peace, Amen.

(Minister is Done, Funeral Director takes over)
(Funeral Director gives the family and friends final instructions here.)

More Committal Examples:

Minister: Blessed be the God and Father of our Lord Jesus Christ, who according to His abundant mercy has born us again unto a living hope by the resurrection of Jesus Christ from the dead, Amen.

In sure and certain hope of the resurrection into eternal life through our Lord Jesus Christ, we commend to Almighty God our brother/sister *(full name)* and we commit his/her body to the ground: (with flowers) earth to earth, ashes to ashes, dust to dust. Blessed are they who die in the Lord, they rest from their labors and their works do follow them.

Benediction

Minister: Now unto him who is able to keep you from falling, and to present you faultless before the presence of his glory with exceeding joy, to the only wise God our Savior, be glory and majesty, dominion and power, both now and forever, Amen.

Minister: God our Father and Maker, you made our brother/sister *(full name)*, in your own image; you set his/her feet on our pilgrim trek; you watched over him/her along the way. As you lovingly received and welcomed him/her to the ranks of the redeemed, we pray that you would continue to guide our steps so that at the appointed time, we will join *(full name)* in the communion of saints: forgiven, transformed, and fit for our new life with the Lord Jesus Christ, in whose name we pray, Amen.

Benediction

Minister: The grace of the Lord Jesus Christ, and the love of God, and the sweet communion of the Holy Spirit be with you all, Amen.

Minister: Faithful God, sustain our faith, we pray, in trying times when we are perplexed and in pain. Help us to trust in you that we may be able to entrust our loved ones to your tender care in life, as well as in death, assured of your mercy, filled with hope by your promise of new life beyond the gates of death. Let your Holy Spirit, the Comforter, endow our hearts with strength to go on, enriched by the memory of *(full name)*, secure in your love. In the mighty and matchless name of Jesus Christ, Amen.

Benediction

Minister: Yea, though I walk through the valley of the shadow of death, I will fear no evil, for Thou art with me, thy rod and thy staff they comfort me, Amen.

Funeral Scriptures

Additional Old Testament Funeral Scriptures:

NAHUM 1:7

The Lord is good, a refuge in times of trouble; He cares for those who trust in Him.

ISAIAH 43:1-3

"Fear not, for I have redeemed you; I have called you by your name; you are mine. When you pass through the waters, I will be with you; and through the rivers, they will not sweep over you. When you walk through the fire, you will not be burned, the flames will not set you ablaze. For I am the Lord your God, the Holy One of Israel, your Savior; . . .

ISAIAH 54:8, 10

…"with everlasting kindness I will have compassion on you, says the Lord, your Redeemer. Though the mountains be shaken and the hills be removed, yet my unfailing love for you will not be shaken, nor my covenant of peace be removed," says the Lord, who has compassion on you.

ISAIAH 41:10

Fear not, for I am with you; be not dismayed, for I am your God. I will strengthen you and help you, I will uphold you with my righteous right hand.

PSALM 68:19

Blessed be the Lord, Who daily loads us with benefits, The God of our salvation! . . .

PSALM 46:1-2

God is our refuge and strength, a very present help in trouble. Therefore we will not fear...

PSALM 91:1-9 NKJ

He who dwells in the secret place of the Most High shall abide under the shadow of the Almighty.

I will say of the Lord, "He is my refuge and my fortress; My God, in Him I will trust." Surely He shall deliver you from the snare of the fowler and from the perilous pestilence. He shall cover you with His feathers, and under His wings you shall take refuge; His truth shall be your shield and buckler. You shall not be afraid of the terror by night, nor of the arrow that flies by day, nor of the pestilence that walks in darkness, nor of the destruction that lays waste at noonday.

A thousand may fall at your side, and ten thousand at your right hand; but it shall not come near you. Only with your eyes shall you look, and see the reward of the wicked. Because you have made the Lord, who is my refuge, even the Most High, your habitation.

Additional New Testament Funeral Scriptures:
JOHN 16:33 NKJ

"These things I have spoken to you, that in me you may have peace. In this world you will have tribulation; but be of good cheer, I have overcome the world."

JOHN 14:27 NKJ
"Peace I leave with you, my peace I give to you; not as the world gives do I give to you. Let not your heart be troubled, neither let it be afraid.

JOHN 11:25 NKJ
Jesus said to her, "I am the resurrection and the life. He who believes in me, though he may die, he shall live.

ROMANS 8:34-35, 37-39 NKJ
Who is he who condemns? It is Christ who died, and furthermore is also risen, who is even at the right hand of God, who also makes intercession for us. Who shall separate us from the love of Christ? Shall tribulation, or distress, or persecution, or famine, or nakedness, or peril, or sword? Yet in all these things we are more than conquerors through Him who loved us. For I am persuaded that neither death nor life, nor angels nor principalities nor powers, nor things present nor things to come, nor height nor depth, nor any other created thing, shall be able to separate us from the love of God which is in Christ Jesus our Lord.

2 CORINTHIANS 1:3-4 NKJ
Blessed be the God and Father of our Lord Jesus Christ, the Father of mercies and God of all comfort, who comforts us in all our tribulation…

PHILIPPIANS 1:21, 23 NIV
For to me, to live is Christ, and to die is gain. For I am torn between the two, I desire to depart and be with Christ, which is better by far.

Cremation

While the Church generally still prefers burial or entombment after the manner of Christ's own burial, out of respect for the human body and belief in the Resurrection, cremation may be chosen for sufficient reason. Though the Scriptures never refer to cremation directly, each minister will have to consider cremation through prayer, a matter of conscience, and the leading of the Holy Spirit. There are some general considerations to keep in mind when facing the question of cremation.

Cremation may be requested for hygienic, economic, or other reasons of a public or private nature. Some examples would be: transfer of the remains to a distant place, possible avoidance of considerable expense, national tradition or custom, or a severe psychological or pathological fear of burial in the ground on the part of the deceased. When cremation is seen as an acceptable alternative to the normal manner of burial, the various elements of the funeral service should remain the same.

People do many different things with cremated remains. Some scatter the remains, some keep them at home and some leave the remains at the crematorium or the funeral home. Some choose burial or inurnment in a cemetery. The Church recommends burial or inurnment of cremated remains as a mark of respect for the human body which was a temple of the Holy Spirit and will share in the Resurrection. Again, the final decision will be up to the immediate family.

The remains of cremated bodies should be treated with the same respect given to the corporal remains of a human body. This includes the manner in which they are carried, the care and attention to appropriate placement and transport, and their final disposition. Whenever possible, appropriate means of memorializing the deceased should be utilized, such as a plaque or stone that records the name of the deceased. Memorials are an important aid to survivors, providing a focal point for the expression of grief and a place of comfort as survivors go through the grieving process.[68]

If a cremation service is to be performed by a Christian minister or leader, you can simply follow the funeral liturgy and guidelines as well as the benediction and interment starting on page 149. Customize the service using your own words. This can be carried out at the funeral home, in a mausoleum, cemetery, at someone's home or at an outside location.

Dedications and Installations

First and foremost, Christians are to dedicate themselves, their children, and their possessions to God. Your first tithe is to present yourself in service to God (2 Corinthians 8:5). Acts of dedication may be performed in private by the individual, by the family, or other small group. This may also be done in a public service of dedication by the entire congregation. The choice of appropriate Scripture passages, music, prayers, and other materials can contribute to the effectiveness of the occasion. A certain amount of formal planning and order is essential. All such dedication services should be conducted with dignity and reverence in keeping with the worship of God. **The following suggestions are offered:**

1. All persons rightfully belong to God. They are truly His, only when they willingly commit themselves to Him. Paul said, *"Do you not know that your body is a temple of the Holy Spirit, who is in you, whom you have received from God? You are not your own; you were bought at a price. Therefore honor God with your body."* – 1 Corinthians 6:19-20

2. Throughout history God's people have practiced dedication of themselves and their possessions. Biblical examples include: Altars - Numbers 7:10-11, Vessels of Service - 1 Kings 7:51, Temple of Worship - 1 Kings 8:63, The Wall of Jerusalem - Nehemiah 12:27, Private Dwellings - Deuteronomy 20:5, Person's - Aaron - Exodus 28:3, Samuel - 1

Samuel 1:21-28, Priests - Ezra 8:23-30, Jesus - Luke 2:22-35, Paul and Barnabas - Acts 13:2-3, Deacons - Acts 6:1- 6.
3. Dedication services are definite acts of worship and should be planned so as to bring honor to God and solemn commitment of persons and things to His service.
4. There are no set forms or ceremonies which must be followed. There is room for variety and creativity to suit the particular occasion which will be a transforming experience for those in attendance.[69]

Dedication of a Church Building

A church dedicatory service is a sacred occasion and if properly planned and carried out, inspires greater respect for the house of God. He will acknowledge this gift and fill His house with His presence. God's dwelling place on earth should be regarded just as holy as God's dwelling place in heaven. *There is no value in dedicating a house to the Lord if His Presence is not respected.* On the day of dedication, we expect the Lord to fill this house with His glory just as He did the Tabernacle of Israel. The words God spoke to Israel remain binding today: "Let them make me a sanctuary; that I may dwell among them." We build a church *for* God, but by the dedication we give it *to* God. His house of worship is holy, not only on Sunday morning, but every hour of every day of the week.

Prior to the dedication, all participants should

be clearly informed as to their participation in the program and the order of service. A printed program should also be prepared well in advance and given to each attendant. It is appropriate to have several ministers present, and if possible, representatives from your conference and possibly the mayor of your town or even the State Governor. If appropriate within your tradition, the news media can also be informed and invited. You may be surprised by their positive response. Inviting the media is an excellent method of spreading the news of your new church, but more importantly the Good News of the Gospel.

The entire program should leave a lasting impression of the sacredness of God's presence in His temple.[70]

The following is a suggested program for a New Church Dedicatory Service:

- ❏ Prelude
- ❏ Congregation Rises as Ministers Approach the Platform
- ❏ Announcements by Pastor
- ❏ Special Music
- ❏ Scripture Reading
- ❏ Prayer
- ❏ Church History (possibly the financial statement)
- ❏ Special Music
- ❏ Dedicatory Sermon
- ❏ Offertory
- ❏ Presentation of Deed to Conference by Elder of the Church
- ❏ Closing Song
- ❏ Benediction

Blessing a Home

The home is God's gift to the family and to society. It is His desire that our home be dedicated to Him. This is our Christian privilege and duty which brings honor to God.

Therefore, most importantly, the minister must be invited by the owners to dedicate their home and themselves to God. You do not ask someone if you can visit their home and bless it for them. Part of the dedication process is the willing and faithful choice the homeowners (or renters) make out of their desire to have the blessing ad*ministered*.

Once invited, the minister arrives at the designated time and greets each member of the family. Then holding hands in a circle, the minister prays the prayer that follows. Immediately after the prayer, the minister uses Holy Oil to anoint *all* the entryways of the home. This includes the garage, the bulkhead to the basement and the main entryways to the building if the home is part of a larger complex or structure. Apply the oil with the right index finger in the shape of the cross. Put it on the molding or ledge above the door. As it is applied say, "Protect and save in the Name of Jesus Christ." Tell the owners not to wipe the oil off or remove it. Also, anoint the headboards of all the beds in each bedroom, and before leaving, ask if there are any prayer requests from the family for specific needs.

Sample Home Blessing Prayer:

Reading: *Unless the Lord builds the house, its builders labor in vain. Unless the Lord watches over the city, the watchmen stand guard in vain.* – Psalm 127:1

Prayer: Father, Lord Jesus, Holy Spirit, we acknowledge You this day. We understand that all of our help is in the name of the Lord, Who has made heaven and earth. We humbly beg of You, God the Father almighty, to bless and sanctify this home, those who live in it and everything in it and all that happens here. Be so kind as to fill it with all good things. Grant them, Lord, abundance of blessings from heaven and the substance of life from the richness of the earth. Direct the longings of their prayer to the fruit of Your mercy. Lord, bless and sanctify this home with Your Presence, as You are welcome in this place. May all who enter feel love and caring and may they ask, "What must I do to be saved?" May Your Holy Spirit live within the walls of this house, guard it and all who live in it, in the name of Jesus Christ our Lord, Amen."

Dedication of a Baby or Child

The dedication service of a child is actually a promise by the parents to offer their child (usually in infancy) to God and to dedicate themselves to the rearing of the child for the glory of God. It should be understood that this act of dedication is not a sacrament or church ordinance, nor does it impart salvation to the child. Ceremonial acts, such as baptism, the laying on of hands, and so forth, are not appropriate for a baby dedication service. It is a recognition that the life of the child is a gift from God and an acknowledgement that the child's life rightfully belongs to God.

This is not a baptism. Baptism is a matter of personal choice following an individual's free will acceptance of Jesus Christ as their Lord and Savior. The individual must, of course, reach a certain age and maturity to understand this decision with all the responsibilities and meaning.

In the Bible, Hannah dedicated her baby boy Samuel to God (1 Samuel 1:25-28). Also, the baby Jesus was dedicated by his parents (Luke 2:22-35). This act of worship has been called the "presentation of the child" or the "blessing of the children" (Mark 10:16). The actual act of dedication is often part of a Sunday morning worship service in many Christian churches. At this service, the child is brought before the congregation and the pastor blesses the child with prayer and sometimes a word of prophecy over the child's life. It is a privilege of the church to encourage and assist parents in the proper training and development of their children. This is why it is appropriate for home and church to unite in the service of dedication for parents and children.

At the Child Dedication Service:

1. We first give thanks to God for the creation and birth of the child.
2. We make a solemn promise as parents and a church that by relying on the grace of God and working

together, we will endeavor to provide guidance to the child in Biblical instruction, discipline, salvation experience, and growth in the Lord.
3. We are to pray for God's blessings upon the child in the presence of the Holy Spirit, remembering how the Lord Jesus Christ took little children and blessed them.
4. As the minister, you must decide in your heart and conscience whether you will dedicate children to God whose parents have not confessed Christ as Savior. Remember that regardless, the child belongs to God.

The Commitment of the Parents:

Minister to Parents – Example 1: "In presenting your child to the Lord, do you promise in dependence upon God's grace and upon the partnership of this church, to teach your child the truths of the Christian faith? Will you set a Christian example before him/her, to bring your child up in the instruction and discipline of the Lord and to encourage him/her to accept Christ as his/her Savior under the guidance of the Holy Spirit?" (Parents Response) "We will."

Minister to Parents – Example 2: "Throughout the ages, godly parents have presented their children to the Lord in dedication. You follow a noble heritage. In presenting your child to the Lord, you enter into a solemn relationship with God who keeps this covenant with a 1000 generations. While dedication is a worthy act, it offers no saving virtue. Dedication does not guarantee your child salvation. When they become older, and reach the age of accountability, they must confess Jesus Christ as their personal Savior. Believing this child is a gift from God, and that He shall hold you accountable for him/ her, do you confess that it is your purpose to dedicate this child to the Lord and to His service? Will you pray with your child, instruct him/ her to faithfully adhere to the doctrines of the Christian faith, teach him/ her to read the Word of God, teach him/her to pray and to lead a holy life and to take your child faithfully to the house of worship to attend services and do everything in your power to bring him/ her into the knowledge of Jesus Christ as Savior and Lord?" [71]

(Parents Response) "We will."

Minister to the Congregation – Example 1: "Do you as members of this church, promise to join these parents in the teaching and training of this child that he/she may be led in due time to trust Christ as Savior?"

(Congregation's Response) "We will."

Minister to the Congregation – Example 2: "As a local congregation we bear a responsibility to this family. Will you pray for this family, encourage them as they grow together, and do all that is in your power to assist them in the leading of their child to know Jesus Christ as his/her personal Lord and Savior? If you do, please show that commitment by standing."

(Congregation's Response) All Stand.

Prayer of Dedication:

(Some ministers hold the child in their arms for this prayer or they place their hand on the child's head)

This is a prayer of thanksgiving for the child, a promise to God to be responsible for this young life and a petition to God for His blessings and leadership in the lives of the parents and child.[72]

Prayer of Dedication - Example 1: "I dedicate you, (child's name), to God in the name of the Father and of the Son and of the Holy Spirit. I loose you from the powers of darkness and may your young life be nurtured and matured under the gracious influence of the Holy Spirit. May God protect you physically and deliver you from temptation. May He early call you into His Kingdom and ultimately into His service, using you to advance His glory and to hasten the coming of our Lord Jesus Christ, Amen."

Prayer of Dedication - Example 2: "Father God, in the name of Jesus Christ Your Son, I dedicate this child to you Lord, all the days of his/her life. May Your grace and mercy shine down upon this child and protect them. Grow him/her into a good and godly man/woman, and when it comes their time, may they confess with the lips you have created that Jesus Christ is their Lord and Savior. Bless them now and forever with the dew of heaven, in Jesus name, Amen."

Following the prayer of dedication, some pastors seal the blessing with a kiss to the child's forehead. This is a very special moment for parents, grandparents, relatives, friends and the entire congregation.

Single Parents:

Single parent families are simply a matter of fact in our changing society. If the parent offering his or her child has sole responsibility for the child's upbringing, there is no reason not to solemnize the parent's desire to dedicate their child to the Lord. If the absent parent maintains some custodial right to the child, and he or she is not in agreement with the covenant of dedication, the minister will need to exercise careful discretion before consenting to dedicate the child.

Remember, with all child dedications, any and all information will be later entered into church records and upon a certificate that the minister gives to the parents during or following the service.[73]

Installation Service for a Pastor/Leader

An installation service for church leaders is always appropriate and may be quite meaningful. The purpose is the dedication and commitment of the elected persons to their offices of responsibility. The services may be designed for the installation of a new pastor, associate minister, officer, teacher, deacon, volunteer leader or any other paid staff member. This can be done at any time during the calendar year. A special Sunday afternoon service is always good. Some churches may elect to install a church leader during an actual Sunday worship service.

The installation service should take place as soon as possible after the new pastor or leader arrives or is appointed. Usually, a committee is assigned for the installation service. This committee may be directed by the pastor, district superintendent, or local conference. Many installation services have the pastor/leader consecrated and installed just following the sermon. It is an appropriate time and a very powerful moment during the congregation's worship.

Suggested Order of Installation Service:

- ❏ Musical Prelude
- ❏ Congregation Rises (ministers approach the platform)
- ❏ Prayer
- ❏ Scripture Reading (or responsive reading)

- ❏ Welcome by the Moderator (District Superintendent, President of Conference, Bishop, Area Pastor)
- ❏ Special Music (2 songs)
- ❏ Sermon of Installation
- ❏ Consecration of Incoming Pastor/Leader (new pastor/leader and wife kneeling, anointing oil, laying on of hands by bishop, area pastors, receiving of certificate)
- ❏ Charge to New Pastor (attending official)
- ❏ Response (from new pastor)
- ❏ Love Offering (to new pastor)
- ❏ Closing Song
- ❏ Benediction (congregation standing)

Wording for the Charge to the New Pastor:

Bishop/Moderator: "Pastor (name), this is a service of personal dedication to your task. During these sacred moments, have you considered the particular Call of God that has come to you for such a time as this and will you will allow God's Holy Spirit to remind you of the divine resources available to you for your work? Do you sincerely believe that you have been led by the Holy Spirit of God to engage in this work and to assume its responsibilities?"

New Pastor: "Yes, I do so believe."

Bishop/ Moderator to the Congregation: "Do you the congregation affirm this leader? Do you pledge to him/her your support and prayers?"

Congregation in Unison: "We do." [74]

Pastoral Counseling

What is Pastoral Counseling?

Pastoral counseling differs from secular psychological counseling in that it helps people to heal through the power of the Holy Spirit and the knowledge of their salvation through Christ's death on the cross as payment for their sins. The person seeking counsel comes to the understanding that God is faithful and just to forgive their sins and to cleanse them from all unrighteousness (1 John 1:9).

The value of counseling by a pastor is multi-faceted. Pastoral counseling is often provided by a church pastor to an individual or couple in their own flock. This brings a close connection between the counselor and those seeking assistance. Using a Biblical-based discussion, the minister offers profound insight into the way sin affects human personality, and how confession and taking responsibility will restore the individual to wholeness in Christ. Biblical-based counseling also offers guidance to divine strength and healing for those who seek counseling in which they have been hurt by the sin of another person.

Guiding Principles

First, counseling is part of a pastor's job description. As a shepherd, the minister's duties include feeding, protecting, and caring for those in one's congregation. Just as a shepherd must bind up the wounds of the sheep that are sick or injured, so does the church pastor bind and soothe the emotional wounds suffered by those in their flock.

Second, pastoral counseling uses the truths of Scripture, explaining and applying them to the individual's life. Exhorting, rebuking, correcting, and training so that practical help is gained through the understanding and application of God's Word (2 Timothy 3:16). The Word of God has a power not gained from textbooks or taking courses in psychology, but has the power to "penetrate even to dividing soul and spirit, joints and marrow; it judges the thoughts and attitudes of the heart" (Hebrews 4:12). The Word is the pastor's primary tool in counseling, and through years of study, they are in a unique position to wield the sword of truth.

Third, the pastor has a relationship with those they counsel that continues outside the counseling sessions. The minister is in a uniquely helpful position to observe and follow the progress of the church members they counsel. Also, the pastoral counselor can, with extraordinary discretion, solicit the prayers and advice of others in the church such as associate ministers, elders, and deacons.

Fourth, there is a strong accountability factor that the pastor can bring to bear during counseling sessions. Christian counseling, by its definition, brings God into the healing and correction process. Unlike secular counseling in which the individual is working for their own personal benefit, Christian

Cautions in Pastoral Counseling:

There are some downsides to pastoral counseling, but the effect is minimal as compared to the healing and transformation received.

First, the average, modern-day pastor is overwhelmed with many tasks and must be careful not to take on more than they can handle. Many churches spread counseling out among associate pastors or elders who are equally equipped to counsel from the Word of God. Some churches hire counseling pastors whose primary role is to counsel those in need from within the congregation, freeing the preaching pastor for sermon preparation and teaching responsibilities.

Second, care must be taken to avoid counseling situations that can lead to sin. Male pastors should not counsel women individually without another person present, preferably another woman, perhaps the pastor's wife (More on the subject of immorality amongst Christian ministers in Rev. Dr. Michael Morawski's book, *Dis-Grace: Immorality of Christian Leaders and How to Prevent It*).

Discernment should also be exercised to be certain a dependent relationship does not occur between the pastor and those they counsel. Dependence upon God and His Word should be sought and stressed in each session, not dependence on the pastor to meet every emotional and spiritual need, an impossible task for anyone.

Third, strongly consider liability insurance. We live in a litigious culture. Even if the minister has done all things correctly within the counseling practice, they are not immune from being sued. The very process of answering a lawsuit is time consuming and expensive. Insurance allows you to be somewhat freed from the damages of this ever-present threat.[75]

Advantages of Pastoral Counseling

When reading of those who had negative behavioral patterns (sins) that Paul listed for the Corinthian church, we are reminded of people in our culture today who exhibit the exact same destructive behaviors throughout their lives (1 Corinthians 6:1-11). But then Paul said, "And that is what some of you were" (1 Corinthians 6:11). When these people came to Christ, He not only saved them, but they were delivered from the sins that bound them. They came out of a world controlled by the devil and became a part of a healthy community. In spite of the Corinthian's problems, it was still a church body of Spirit-filled people who ministered to one another.[76]

The majority of people in our communities turn to a pastor or priest when they have a crisis or counseling need. Robert Morgan wrote: "Pastoral counseling is best done by a pastor–not a professional counselor or psychotherapist. Good professional Biblical counselors certainly play an important role when the complexities of mental illness are involved, but they are allies of the pastor, not substitutes for him." [77]

Morgan listed several advantages pastors have in counseling:

1. Friendship – Those who need help are counseling with a friend, not just a professional.
2. Prior Relationship – In many cases, there has been an ongoing relationship between the person and the pastor. The pastor often knows the family's history, spiritual maturity, and past crisis experiences.
3. Preaching – Preaching can include Biblical counseling from the pulpit.
4. Biblical Advice – People want to know what the Bible says about their particular need.
5. Availability – Typically, pastors are much more accessible to their parishioners. It is important for people who have lived in destructive behavioral patterns to become a part of a caring church, pastored by a caring pastor. This kind of community is healthy and is an encouragement to those coming out of spiritually or physically harmful lifestyles.[78]

At times, part of the care leaders offer people is helping them find a competent Christian mental health professional. My rule of thumb has always been that if I sense mental illness, serious depression, or suicidal thinking, I automatically refer to a Christian mental health professional, and I remain their pastor. Even for those I refer, I still pray for them and meet with them for pastoral counseling. However, I believe that the professional has the expertise to handle the complicated and delicate issues that come up with these types of difficulties.

Remember these 10 key realities when you are involved in Pastoral Counseling:

1. *The Scripture is always right.* The Bible covers a myriad of problems, difficulties, and issues that people face every day. We know how God feels about divorce, adultery, substance abuse, dishonesty, and numerous other harmful behaviors. Scripture is clear about God's desire to set people free, forgive them of their sins, and restore their lives. The Bible is our blueprint for living and should be every pastor's counseling manual.

2. *The person being counseled is always responsible to do what is right.* None of us can blame others for our personal choices in life. It is the choice of the person being counseled whether they make the right or wrong decision. You can pray for and encourage those who come for counseling, but in the end it is their decision. The pastoral counselor is responsible *to* the counselee, not *for* them.

3. *There is always a Biblical, Christ-honoring response that the counselee is capable of choosing.* What is the right thing to do when a person has wronged you? Every issue a person faces in life has a Christ-honoring response. It might be a difficult but necessary confrontation, a gentle rebuke, or forgiveness.

4. *Listen carefully.* What is said and what is meant may be different. Often people will hint at their situation,

but never clearly state it. As you listen, try to uncover the subtext and hear what they are really saying. Ask questions such as: "Am I hearing you say…?" or "Is there something else you want to talk about?" This type of question often prompts the person to bring out the real issues.

5. *Do not be afraid to ask about willful sin.* If you suspect sinful behavior, ask about it at the appropriate time. You could say: "Have you been seeing someone else?" or "What behaviors have you been involved in that you know God would not approve of?"

6. *The counselee is a person of worth, made in the image of God.* No matter what people have done, they are important to God and should be important to us. God can cleanse, redeem, and restore anyone who comes to Him for help. Your role is to counsel, not to judge.

7. *Counseling advice should be specific and doable.* When you give people advice about how to overcome their problems, be specific about how to do it. Write out a "road map" for them. Just instructing them to stop a certain behavior won't work. They often know they need to stop, but they don't know how. You can help them find the "how" by equipping them with the skills and tools they need.

8. *Remain hopeful, but realize there are no instant cures to life's problems.* Any habit that has lasted years will often take months or years to overcome. A bad marriage doesn't become a good marriage overnight. Those who have grown up in an abusive home could have similar challenges with their family. Be patient with people, and remain hopeful. Be an encourager. Let them know with full assurance that God will get them through.

9. *Know that God can use you.* Take charge. There are a variety of people and problems you will face in ministry. Help, in some way, those who cross your path. It might be through counseling, or it could be through referral to a Christian mental health professional or medical doctor. God will help you work with the people He has placed under your care.

10. *You are a person talking to a person.* Counseling is a relationship. Let people know that God has helped you with your difficulties and challenges. This gives people hope and lets them know that you are also working out your salvation with "fear and trembling."

Counseling is a part of every pastor's life. We counsel after a tragedy, at a funeral, during a marriage difficulty, or in a premarital counseling session. We counsel in the church foyer, during visitation, or before a critical surgery. Ministers are servants, period.[79]

Remember to be balanced between your counseling and other clerical duties. Decide ahead of time how many sessions you will give each congregant. You may find that four or five sessions per week, each lasting 30 to 45 minutes, is an enormous load on your schedule. Remember to discuss the length of each session as well as the number of times you will meet with the counselee prior to the first session.

Sometimes couples feel guilty after pastoral counseling. They feel when the pastor preaches, it sounds as if he or she is telling part of their story to the congregation and sometimes they leave the church. There is no need for the people to pour out all the details of their sins to you when counseling. It might help them, but it may pollute your mind in the process.

Before you meet for each session, pray for wisdom, guidance, and protection.

Also, be careful as a pastor when counseling one spouse without the other being present. Why? Your counsel may come between the couple and create more of a rift. It may also turn one spouse against the other. Therefore, it is wise to counsel with both people present.

If an unmarried member of the opposite sex asks you for counseling, or if a married member of the opposite sex is seeking your counsel about issues other than their relationship, you should ask your spouse to counsel either with you, or have your spouse or some other qualified person of the same sex counsel them. For instance, Titus 2:3-4 clearly sets the pattern of older women in the church counseling the younger women.

Remember, just because God has brought a person in need to your office, does not mean that you personally are to address their needs. Prayerfully consider those in your congregation who are trustworthy and who have the gifts, wisdom, maturity and Biblical knowledge to offer appropriate counseling. Gender, age, and other factors must be considered in the sacred space of counseling in the name of Jesus Christ. Other pastors, stronger than yourself, have been drawn into adulterous affairs with congregants they were "counseling." Sometimes it is best not to counsel with the opposite sex at all.[80]

Substance Abuse Counseling

Clergy and other pastoral ministers need to be effective in providing care to families and individuals who are troubled by alcohol or drug problems. The core competencies presented as essential components for clergy and pastoral ministers in meeting the needs of persons struggling with substance abuse, and their family members, are as follows:

1. Be aware of the generally accepted definition of alcohol and other drug dependencies and the societal stigma attached to alcohol and other drug abuse.
2. Be knowledgeable about the signs of alcohol and other drug dependence; characteristics of withdrawal; effects on the individual and the family, and characteristics of the stages of recovery.
3. Be aware that possible indicators of the disease may include, among others: marital conflict, family violence (physical, emotional, and verbal), suicide, hospitalization, or encounters with the criminal justice system.
4. Understand that addiction erodes and blocks religious and spiritual development; and be able to effectively communicate the importance of faith, spirituality and the practice of religion in recovery, using the Scriptures, traditions, and rituals of the faith community.
5. Be aware of the potential benefits of early intervention for the addicted person, their family, children, and career, etc.

6. Be aware of appropriate pastoral interactions with the addicted person as well as all those affected by their addiction. This can extend far beyond their family and friends.
7. Be able to communicate and sustain an appropriate level of concern, and messages of hope and caring.
8. Be familiar with and utilize available community resources to ensure a continuum of care for the addicted person and their family. Have a general knowledge of, and where possible, exposure to the 12-step programs such as: AA, NA, Al-Anon, Nar-Anon, Alateen, ACOA, and other groups.
9. Be able to acknowledge and address values, issues, and attitudes regarding alcohol and other drug use and dependence in yourself and within your own family.
10. Be able to shape, form, and educate a caring congregation that welcomes and supports persons and families affected by alcohol and other drug dependence.
11. Be aware of how prevention strategies can benefit the larger community.

Pastoral counselors have a significant capacity to enhance the health and well-being of individuals, families, and communities. Pastoral counselors wanting to help should work with behavioral health providers, and organizations like the Johnson Institute and NACoA who will be able to provide the necessary knowledge and skills to religious leaders in the areas of screening, referral, pastoral care, and community education to help those affected by alcoholism and addiction to find care, treatment, and effective recovery support.

There is a significant need for training to help congregational ministers obtain this knowledge and integrate these skills into the daily practice of their ministry. At the same time, there is a tremendous unmet need for addiction treatment in this country. It is estimated that of persons aged 12 or older, 7.7 million need treatment for an illicit drug problem and 18.6 million need treatment for an alcohol problem. Only 1.4 million individuals have received treatment at a specialty substance abuse facility (SAMHSA, 2003).[81]

Pastoral counseling can and does make a difference. To be truly effective, you must first and fully know yourself as a minister of Jesus Christ. Under no circumstances, should a minister attempt to counsel people with problems beyond their training and ability. You might even consider putting together your own directory of counseling services in your area for different levels of referral. Remember, we reproduce what we are. Train other ministers coming up behind you. It is the smart and effective minister who delegates.

Hospital and Home Visits

The ministry of shepherding or simply the care of souls is a major area of your life's work. Am I my brother's keeper? Yes! All church members are responsible for the well-being of one another. Jesus Himself went about doing good, giving support, guidance and healing many troubled people, and He instructed us to do the same.

Today's leader must also invest a great deal of time visiting people in hospitals and their homes. Many are sick, dying, grieving, shut-in, elderly, anxious, fearful, guilt-ridden, and forsaken. The modern day leader must make use of their time and possess a knowledge of spiritual resources in meeting people's diverse needs. The following principles are meant to aid the minister and other church leaders in performing this vital ministry.

Visitation and Care Ministry Principles:
1. **Prayer.** Prayer is the foundational lifeline to the care ministry. A leader must be bathed in prayer so they will be speaking and operating in the power of the Holy Spirit, not one's own flesh.
2. **The pastor cannot do it all.** One should organize, train, and encourage other church leaders to assist in bearing one another's burdens.
3. **Afternoon visitation hours are best.** The pastor's morning is spent in creative study, planning, and prayer, while the afternoon is reserved for visitation and counseling.

4. **Emergency cases will always interrupt normal schedules.** As a minister, always be prepared for the unexpected. Be ready to go at a moment's notice. Keep what you might need in your car at all times.
5. **Visitations should be purposeful and specific.** Prepare your spirit along with relevant materials, facts about the person and their condition, choice of Scripture verses, guiding thoughts, and prayers to be used.
6. **Master interpersonal communication.** During a hospital or home visit, ministers and leaders cannot effectively bring the faith-filled comfort necessary without proper communication skills. While common sense must prevail, be aware of the flow of the Holy Spirit. If you do this, you will not attempt to force a person to respond a certain way. You are bringing the Word and opening the door to the healing power of the Holy Spirit.
7. **Know the Word.** The Bible is the minister's anchor in times of trouble. There are times when only the Bible's words can bring comfort.[82]
8. **Lead people to Christ.** When the doctor has indicated to the minister there is not much time left, make sure to explain the Gospel slowly and clearly and lead the person to salvation. When people are dying, do not ask if they are saved. They are fearful and will not tell the truth. Instead, ask this vital question from Dr. D. James Kennedy's *Evangelism Explosion* course:

If you were to die today and stand before God, and He were to ask you, "Why should I let you

into my heaven, what would you say?"
Their answer exposes their belief about their salvation and will usually come in 1 of 3 categories:
a. **They will be speechless.** They do not know how to answer or what they would say to God.
b. **They defend their salvation with works.** They point out how they were a church worker, they love God, they have great faith, never killed anyone, never robbed a bank, etc.
c. **Jesus.** Just Jesus. Not Jesus plus anything else. Only Jesus can save and Him alone. His sacrifice on the cross paid our entry way into heaven. If you are with someone on the verge of death, this one single truth may lead them to spending eternity in their rightful place with God in heaven.

Modern Day Stressors

Today, the ministry of visitation has never been more difficult, nor has it been more needed. People everywhere are busy and stressed. It is a challenge to find people in their homes calm enough to benefit from your visit. People are overwhelmed beyond the breaking point. The thought of a visit from "the minister" is not necessarily a source or time of healing and growth, but just another source of stress!

In addition, people today are more cautious of those in the ministry than they were in past generations. Negative, damaging stories about ministers failing and falling have been pervasive for decades. Moreover, the

Internet and social media have clouded our perception of people and broken down our trust level to a lowly cynicism. Our minds are bombarded with images and slogans until we cannot even think for ourselves. People are suspicious. Everyone is fearful because of the threat of accusations and lawsuits, either from the government, neighbors, co-workers, bystanders, or from the very person one seeks to help. The devil has turned the genders against each other, the races against each other, and social classes against each other. He is sitting back and enjoying just watching us destroy ourselves.[83]

Remember, Jesus is Lord. Have courage and compassion. Clearly and authentically demonstrate that the person to whom you are speaking is of great importance to you. Don't judge. Listen openly. Respond to their pain with God's love. Be patient with them. Pray continually...and all obstacles will eventually fall away.

Visitation Benefits

✝

Individuals must know that theirs is a church and a minister who are offering and demonstrating the love of Christ. **The pastor who maintains a successful visitation ministry will reap rich dividends:**
- ❏ They will have a more loyal following.
- ❏ Their sermons will apply more practically to people's lives.
- ❏ Their church will grow numerically.

- As the leader ministers, they will find themselves being ministered to and uplifted.
- Congregational trust level increases.
- Volunteer participation increases.
- Church programs have greater meaning.
- Satisfaction will be forthcoming.

Other Hospital/Home Visit Guidelines

✝

- Increase the efficiency of your ministry by planning hospital and home visits on a convenient route.
- Give people the courtesy of a telephone call so they can get their homes/room prepared.
- Bring several Communion kits with you to administer the Lord's Supper. Don't get caught in a situation where you have to use crackers and water, though these will work.
- When visiting, remember people matter. They are expecting comfort and answers from clergy. Focus on their needs, questions and concerns. Be a good listener. Sometimes silence is best, especially when any words will fall short. This question works in any situation, *"How are you holding up?"* Ask it with meaning and interest. Let them know you truly want an answer.
- Always look for an opportunity to quickly turn a discussion to spiritual considerations. Avoid conversation which could lead them to think

you are only interested in what they could do for the church.
- ❑ Ask the Holy Spirit to bring Scriptures to mind that meet their specific needs.
- ❑ Pray for the family, identifying each member by name, putting them in touch with the God who answers prayer.
- ❑ Depending on your schedule, visits can be anywhere from five minutes to an hour. You must be very sensitive to those who are suffering.
- ❑ Proper dress is usually a good idea. The minister's appearance compliments their presence.
- ❑ If the visit reveals a larger problem, do not leap into a counseling session right there. Instead suggest another time in a few days.
- ❑ The minister's procedure will be determined in part by the patient's physical condition.
- ❑ Be respectful of their time as well. Always arrive on time as a servant of God.
- ❑ After Scripture reading and prayer, ask them if they have any further questions.
- ❑ Visits are not limited to those who are obviously ill or suffering. For instance, when someone in your church has experienced a divorce, they may appreciate a listening ear.
- ❑ Sometimes a home visit for new members can also be very beneficial.
- ❑ Know when to leave. Then, depart with as few words as possible. Politely excuse yourself, as you are an ambassador of Christ's love. There is no need for small talk or awkward departures.[84]

Conflict Resolution

Conflict is nothing more than a situation in which two or more people desire something. They perceive it as being attainable by one or the other, but not by both. There are three basic kinds of conflict: conflict of emotions, conflict of values, and conflict of needs. These conflicts arise from our humanity and strong wills. Conflict is inevitable when people of different values, beliefs, quirks, and backgrounds come together, especially if one or both do not know Christ. Regarding conflict with an unbeliever, pastor and author Max Lucado said, "What do you expect someone walking around in darkness to act like?"

Ministry conflict tests a leader's personal maturity. What we truly are is revealed in a crisis. Conflict processing is important for its value in revealing character. What one *is* in conflict is much more critical than what one *does*. All Christian leaders minister out of who they are in the Lord, rather than what they know. God uses conflict in general to develop inner life maturity. Leadership backlash is a form of integrity testing in which the leader's actual motivation can be revealed. J. Robert Clinton says all leaders will experience conflict stemming from backlash:

"Leadership backlash tests a leader's perseverance, clarity of vision, and faith. Leadership backlash is the negative reactions of followers, other leaders within the group, and Christians outside the group to a course of action taken by the leader once ramifications develop from his decision." [85]

A wise leader sees conflict as primarily supernatural in its source and essence (Ephesians 6:12). Your focus is to depend on God's power to solve the problem in such a way that your leadership capacity, particularly your spiritual authority, is demonstrated and expanded. A leader knows it is imperative to study Scripture, which reveals important principles regarding spiritual warfare. Some physical situations may well be caused, controlled, or instigated by spiritual forces. During this testing period, submission to God's prompting is key. The Apostle Peter said *"Submit yourselves for the Lord's sake to every authority instituted among men: whether to the king, as the supreme authority."* – 1 Peter 2:13

Each church has a staff hierarchy. The pastor hears from God and delegates authority to their subordinates, such as an assistant pastor, new member's pastor, minister of music, etc. The Apostle Paul said, *"Everyone must submit himself to the governing authorities, for there is no authority except that which God has established. The authorities that exist have been established by God."* – Romans 13. Therefore, when someone rebels and conflicts arise, they are rebelling against God.

One of the first steps to resolving conflict is to realize the problem might reside within the minister. When we allow people into our lives who are different in any way from ourselves, it will change us. As leaders, we understand and accept that the way to finally make peace with ourselves and others, thereby acquiring healthy personhood (emotionally, physically, relationally, spiritually) is to pursue ongoing, relentless change and growth.

"The highest reward for a person's toil is not what they get for it, but what they become by it."
- *John Rushkin*

"Every test in our life makes us bitter or better. Every challenge comes to make us or break us. The choice is ours whether we become victim or victor."
- *Unknown*

As your staff grows, it must become even more organized. Job descriptions should be written, signed, and accepted by all incoming staff members. Human resources must be managed systematically; hierarchy and organizational structure must be implemented; expectations must be clear; and conflicts must be recognized and addressed early. Finally, it is wise to add one final duty to every job description: "and any other assignment made by the pastor or his designee." [86]

Conflict Resolution Process

The Gospel of Matthew 18:15-17 gives specific guidelines on how to resolve conflict. You will find divine resolution by applying this method to every conflict you encounter:

If your brother or sister sins against you, go and point out their fault, just between the two of you. If they listen to you, you have won them over. But if they will not listen, take one or two others along, so that 'every matter may be established by the testimony of two or three witnesses.' If they still refuse to listen, tell it to the church; and if they refuse to listen even to the church, treat them as you would a pagan or a tax collector.

To begin the conflict resolution process, follow these steps privately and then with witnesses:

1. **Treat the other person with respect.** (Go privately) Respect for another person is an attitude conveyed by specific behaviors. The way you listen to the other person matters. Looking them in the eyes with compassion while seeking to understand, your tone of voice, your selection of words and the type of reasoning you use all combine to convey your respect or disrespect.

2. **Listen and restate to the other person's satisfaction.** The goal of listening is to understand the content of the other person's point of view, the meaning it has and the feelings the person has about it. Listen to understand, not to form a response.

3. **Briefly state your views, needs and feelings.**
   a. State your point of view briefly.
   b. Select words carefully and avoid criticism or sarcasm.
   c. Say what you mean and mean what you say.
   d. Disclose your feelings and what actions led to you feeling that way.
   e. However, sometimes stating your views, needs, and feelings is not necessary. This could be true when one person is angry and the other is not.

4. **Finally, the pastor has the final say.** You are in charge because the Lord has placed you in this unique position. Do not allow His authority to be

stripped away by conflict, gossip, ridicule, or sabotage. The Bible says when words are many, sin is not absent (Prov. 10:19). When a wheel of your car is out of alignment, it pulls the whole car to one side. The same is true of a person in your ministry out of alignment. It will pull the whole ministry down, and no wheel ever corrects itself. Take action in love.[87]

Connecting Goes Beyond Words

The more you go beyond words, the greater the effectiveness you will have in connecting with people:

One on One

- Connect visually by giving the other person your complete attention (eyes and heart). Turn your body, mind, and heart to theirs.
- Connect intellectually by asking questions, listening carefully, and carefully observing body posture and facial expressions.
- Connect emotionally through safe, gentle touch, but honor boundaries and personal space.

Connecting with a Group

- Connect visually by setting the example. Be relaxed, calm, positive, and open. People in a group will do what they see.
- Connect intellectually by investing in people's growth. Build on what your people already

understand so they can develop to a higher level.
- ❏ Connect emotionally by honoring the group's effort and rewarding its work.

Connecting with an Audience
- ❏ Connect visually by smiling. This lets people know you are happy to be communicating with them.
- ❏ Connect intellectually by pausing strategically to give the audience time to think about something you already said.
- ❏ Connect emotionally through facial expressions, laughter, and tears.
- ❏ Connect individually by addressing the audience as one person. Avoid expressions such as: "Hello everyone," and "How are you all?" Each person is listening as one person, so speak with that focus.

In conflict resolution, adhere to these four key principles to effectively communicate your message:

1. Be prepared
2. Be committed
3. Be interesting
4. Be comfortable [88]

"Even the choicest words lose their power, when they are used to overpower."

- Edwin Friedman

Correct with Love

When correcting someone, remember these ten important principles:

1. Correction is always *for* another person.
2. Correction is to be an affirmation of love and a validation of God. This is referred to as, "affirmation of being."
3. Correction never takes away from their personhood or reduces them in any way.
4. Correction lets the person know how you want the situation to be handled more effectively next time.
5. Correction always asserts their worth as a person and that they are worthy to do this task.
6. Correction clearly communicates what they did well.
7. Wait before acting. Work out your issues and feelings (Matthew 7:3). You can make a situation worse by reacting too quickly or without patient consideration.
8. Keep their self-esteem intact. Do not compare them to anyone else.
9. Never act from a place of defensiveness or with the goal to be right. It will not pay off.
10. A church free of conflict is a sick church. God created us to have free will, with different gifts, goals, and desires. Your objective is to unify your congregation around Jesus Christ. This process will create conflict. Religious organizations without conflict are not churches, they are cults.

How to Live In a Secular World

Be Yourself, Be Real

As a Christian, we are not to hide or conceal our identity as believers, forever fearful of exposing who we are and in Whom we believe. The Lord Himself commanded that we are to be in this world, but not part of it (John 17:14-19). He also reminded us that a city on a hill cannot be hidden (Matthew 7:14). We are to lead people out of darkness into God's marvelous light (1 Peter 2:9). All of this starts with a choice. Right choices equal right results. *"In your hearts set apart Christ as Lord. Always be prepared to give an answer to everyone who asks you to give the reason for the hope that you have. But do this with gentleness and respect."* – 1 Peter 3:15

The Call of every believer is to model grace, not strength. God's desire is to fill His church and His Kingdom with people. He does this by using His disciples and the love they have to draw others to Him (John 13:34-35). Unfortunately, the biggest deterrent to this plan is the very people who love Him. So be wise in how you live. You might be the only Bible some people will ever read.

Most people rarely give thought to the effect they have had or will have on others. When we take a few moments to contemplate how our individual behaviors affect the people with whom we interact each day, we come one step closer to seeing ourselves through the eyes of others. By asking ourselves whether those we encounter walk away feeling appreciated, respected, and liked, we can heighten our awareness of the effect we ultimately have. A simple smile, given freely, can temporarily brighten a person's entire world. Our Jesus-driven conduct may inspire others to consider whether their own lives are reflective of their values. A word of advice can help others see life in an entirely new fashion. Small gestures of kindness can even prove to those embittered by the world that goodness still exists. By simply being ourselves, we influence other's lives in both subtle and life-altering ways.[89]

"Our courageous freedom to be vulnerable and transparent transforms the way we live, love, parent and lead."

— *Brené Brown, Daring Greatly*

"To thine own self be true."
— *Hamlet Act 1, William Shakespeare*

We are not defined by any one thing we do or don't do. Likewise, no one else can define us. It is God who defines us. Life always asks more questions than it provides answers. Therefore, humble yourself before the Almighty, beat your breast like the publican and say, "Lord have mercy on me, a sinner." (Luke 18:13)

This dramatic, turbulent, dynamic, and most often harsh world makes a mockery of our plans and predictions and all that we once were so sure of. It is a world that keeps us on edge, anxious, sleepless, and takes years off our lifespan.

It is a world where nothing makes sense anymore.

Once, we thought we had all the pieces of the puzzle figured out and fitting nicely. Now, they lie disassembled on the floor of our experience. It is a world where we are thrust in directions beyond our control, into the pluralism of all things. Consequently, we are often unable to make peace with the divergent voices we hear daily.

It is a world where ultimate truth no longer wears a single face out in public, and any that suggest that reality does wear a single face is rejected by the majority as nonsensical, even though many of us still believe it. This, and much more, create the chaotic world we personally live in and experience every day of our lives.

To honor and build God's Kingdom, we need to open up and let ourselves be known. We do not need this way of living fully for God to express our feelings, but to guard ourselves against all forces that seek to keep us from Jesus. As we live each day completely for the Savior, the doors keeping us from Him slam shut and the doors to His Kingdom fly open. To bring healing into all of life we need to give concrete expression to the fullness of God's love.

This is the challenge and invitation of the Gospel of Jesus.[90]

"In our solitude as humans, we discover our deep connection with others and with God. When we make ourselves vulnerable, that is when we have the opportunity for true connection, the opportunity to experience love, and the opportunity to realize the point of why we are here."
– Henri Nouwen

Remember To Whom You Belong

We know the word *Gospel* means the good news of Jesus Christ; His birth, life, death, and resurrection. Yet, the Gospel is more than this, because it shows us the love of a Supreme Being, Yahweh, God Almighty, our Father, who sent His Son into the world to die for us (Romans 5:8), even while we were still sinners. That is how much He loves us. This Gospel brings healing, because when you know God loves you and cares for you, it opens you up to grow. So here is a question to ponder: *Are you letting yourself be loved by God?*

Christianity is not a religion, it is a relationship based on faith. By receiving Christ, we have become God's children (John 1:12). When you fully understand and accept that the grace of God is for you, then you can be exactly who you are as an individual, the way God created you, and not an impression we want to give others.

As such, here are important principles to live by:

- ❏ Slow down. Some red lights and yellow ones! – are from God.
- ❏ Learn to be a flexible person. Inflexibility comes from the need to be right. There is no merit in being right, there is only merit in your character.
- ❏ Create an identity of who you *are* that is separate from what you *do*. Be multi-faceted. Leave the church at the church, but take Christ with you everywhere.

- ❑ Never lower your standard of living to fit in. Do not compromise the Word of God while seeking the blessings of God.
- ❑ Do not let anyone or anything take you out of your godly character.
- ❑ Spiritual wisdom can be defined as emotional maturity.
- ❑ Being a believer is not an act, it is a lifestyle.
- ❑ You cannot change others, so refocus the issue back at yourself and ask, "What am I willing to do?"
- ❑ However, sometimes you can *redirect* people's lives.
- ❑ Through your life, the love of God can transform others.
- ❑ Anger is usually a facade for our hurt.
- ❑ Respond from your godly character, rather than reacting from your flesh.
- ❑ People are mostly untrustworthy. Relentless forgiveness is the greatest therapeutic process known to man.

Casting the Vision of Your Church

What is Vision?

A Vision comes from God through the senior pastor. It's the comprehensive statement that tells leaders of the organization in what direction they should move, and what they should accomplish so they can motivate the people under them.

There can be only one vision, anything else is a di-vision.

First, the purpose of the church is determined and then the vision honed from it. Your Vision should be a sentence or two that acts as a guide or slogan for your church. As leaders, you must be firmly convinced of this Vision before you can communicate it effectively to others.

Visions galvanize and motivate people, giving the momentum necessary for equipping the ministry and church for God's glory and purpose.

Ideas in Writing Your Vision:

Read Nehemiah. Notice how Nehemiah's Vision begins, develops, includes, and then how it involves others for clarification and confirmation. How does Nehemiah's Vision compare with yours?

- ❏ Make sure you have a good grasp on the precepts and principles of Scripture.
- ❏ A Vision cannot be written from your will, but only from God's.

- ❏ Remember our sinful nature. Confirm this vision through prayer.
- ❏ The Vision needs to be simple, yet concise.
- ❏ You may not be able to finish it in a short time, at a retreat, or board meeting. It may take months.
- ❏ Vision is the realization of and a response to the working of God.
- ❏ Vision requires us to stretch and change, to learn new skills and to do things out of our comfort zone. This is exactly where you will find Jesus waiting for you.
- ❏ Vision requires you to be a risk taker and have ever increasing faith. You may receive criticism from other well-meaning Christians, leaders, and denominational officials. Listen and educate them on the Biblical precepts and your process.
- ❏ Do not just copy your Vision from another church. You, the leaders, and then the church must go through the honing process. The Vision must fit your church, neighborhood, and place in the Kingdom.
- ❏ Stagnant churches in need of revitalization or those being planted by another church must have a new Vision specific to them in order to grow and take them into a new season.

Casting Your Vision:
- ❏ Casting Vision means empowering your congregation to accept it, live it, and serve in it.
- ❏ Preach the Biblical passage on which your Vision is based with power and conviction. Have people give their testimonies during worship

services on what the Vision means to them and how it manifests in their daily lives.
- At the same time, do not let the Vision consume your church. Keep the focus on the care and love for the people.
- For a Vision to work, it has to be *owned* by the congregation. This is accomplished by educating them on God's Call through Scripture, prayer, patience, encouragement, and the process used to develop the Vision.
- Have your leaders participate in the process as much as possible. They do the fieldwork, the grass roots influencing and implementation of it.
- Personally and positively present the Vision everywhere: in classes, small groups, fellowship gatherings, and in the services.
- Having as many people as possible contribute to the Vision process enables the congregation in the conception and shaping of the Vision. The input of others helps you focus, and consider the various options and needs.
- Make sure you write it out in short, clear, and vivid language so someone who has never seen it will understand it. Have people outside your church look it over for clarity. If a stranger who does not know you or your church can understand and run with it, you may have a winner.

Troubleshooting (when people resist or do not like the plans)
- What are the factors inhibiting the Vision in your church? Are there power plays, political

agendas, the old guard, popularity of the previous pastor/leader, poor Biblical knowledge? How can you solve these issues?

❏ What church traditions and programs should you maintain? Which should you get rid of? How will you go about it without upsetting your congregation? Remember, listing of and educating about the Call and Biblical precepts will be your biggest ally, accompanied by prayer and time.

❏ The fear of change and the unknown is very powerful. People will fight to hold on, and fight to let go. Did you inspire and motivate others to follow you? [91] Trust in God.

Church Membership

The starting point for every church is Jesus Christ. The church's birth was confirmed by the coming of the Holy Spirit (Acts 2:1-11). God also provided the power for its self-perpetuation through witnessing to the world (Acts 1:8).

To be a member of the church is to join the Body of Christ, the community of the redeemed, of which Christ is the Head (Colossians 1:18). It was Christ's love for the church that caused Him to go to the Cross. To be a member of the church is to come under the spiritual covering of Christ and the pastor. The family of God contains people of various ethnicities, culture, classes, and denominational differences. Some churches only take new believers, while other churches receive all walks of life. There may be disagreements of theology, methods and motives, but within the true church, there is a mysterious unity that overrides all divisive factors. Love never fails.[92]

A focus on church membership is important, but not if quality is sacrificed and numbers become the only consideration. Then again, membership must not be neglected thereby allowing the united strength of the church to be lost in the informal relationship of those who gather week after week. Clearly, there is a desirable middle ground.

If spiritual standards of eligibility for membership are to be maintained, a basic procedure is necessary. Even where there are denominational guidelines, the following fundamentals usually apply:

- ❏ Have an established standard of eligibility. The minimum requirement would be satisfactory evidence of regeneration through faith in Christ, conformity to the church beliefs, and acceptance of its constitution and bylaws.
- ❏ Have a properly authorized and trained Intake Team whose responsibility is to meet the needs of new members through a standard process.
- ❏ Members may be received at an altar call, or filling out a private form, at any Sunday worship service or special event the church hosts (Matt. 10:32). Some New Member's Pastors may enroll people privately.
- ❏ The pastor usually announces the reception of new members and will discuss with them their confession of faith.
- ❏ If the new member is known to have membership in another church, the courteous thing to do is to suggest that it be transferred. This can easily be done by the person contacting their former church for a letter of transfer.[93]

Communicate the Benefits of Becoming a Church Member:

1. You place yourself under a spiritual covering because the senior pastor begins to pray for you by name.
2. You become a member of a family. This is not casual, but definite.
3. You outwardly show you have identified with Christ and His followers.

4. You receive the power of the Holy Spirit to go out and be a witness.
5. You encourage others to join by your commitment.
6. You will discover your spiritual gifts and use them to equip others.
7. The Care Ministries can visit you in times of need.
8. You can be baptized and receive an official baptism certificate.
9. You can begin to volunteer in a ministry.
10. Joining a church is Biblical (Hebrews 10:24-25).

Prayers for Certain Occasions

Pastors' and Church Leaders' Prayers:

Father, today I come before you to humble myself. I come before You to yield to Your wisdom and to Your guiding hand. Lord, You must increase and I must decrease if I am to properly shepherd my people. I position myself to be pliable in Your hands this day. In Jesus' name, Amen.

Father God, as a shepherd, I sometimes feel a pull to always be on duty. Wisdom says that even Jesus went away from needy crowds to rest and renew Himself. If Jesus needed it, then how much more will I need it? Help me to realize when I need to rest. Teach me to rest. Help me to realize when I need to spend time building up myself. Teach me to wisely give time to my own spiritual, emotional, mental, and physical needs. Help me to realize when I need to put my family before pastoral requests. Teach me to generously nurture my family. Lord, I ask for wisdom to know the right thing to do and strength to do the right thing. In Jesus' name I pray, Amen.

Father, You are challenging me to rise higher in obedience to You. I will follow you in Jesus' name, Amen.

Father, Lord of my heart, I value You, and I value Your Word. Your Word tells me to love and bless other people.

Your will is for me to view everyone in my life as valuable. You want me to honor people and treat them with respect every day. I receive my mission to love people this day. I receive my mission to be helpful toward their needs, compassionate toward their hurts, encouraging toward their trials, enthusiastic toward their victories, warm toward their presence, and forgiving toward their mistakes and sins. Change my heart, Lord. Teach me to be more like you. I will yield to You this day, in Jesus' name, Amen.

Healing Prayers:

Almighty God and Loving Father, we lift up this beloved one who needs healing. We bring this prayer to you, thanking you for the power of using Your name Jesus, Your blood, and Your Word. We pray in Jesus' name that this person's body will fully receive the strength and healing power of Jesus Christ and that the manifestation of healing will begin this day, Amen.

Heavenly Father, You are our Creator, and You are our Healer. You are Jehovah Rapha - the God who heals. You have compassion for us in our sicknesses and our pain. Your mercy is from everlasting to everlasting. It is not Your will that any of us be sick. I come to you this day, asking You to heal my body. I ask You to go into every cell and correct whatever is wrong. Father, bring healing, harmony, and unity to every organ, and every system of my body. I ask that You would heal the root of any pain that I experience. Thank You that You are repairing everything that has to do with my body.

Right now, I am giving You my fears and my worries. I pick up the shield of faith and draw confidence that You are working on my behalf this day. In Jesus' name, Amen.[94]

Prayer to Break Generational Curses:

Father, I confess the sins of my forefathers that I know about. Sins of _____. I ask You Lord to forgive those who have prayed for my downfall, I ask You Lord to separate me completely from all the sins people have pronounced over me. I command every evil spirit to depart right now by the blood of Jesus. I command any demon afflicting me and my family to leave at once, and I loose wholeness and healing in the name of Jesus Christ. I consider it done in Jesus name, Amen.

Prayer to Spiritually Cleanse a Home:

Heavenly Father, I come to You in the name of Jesus Christ and by the power of His shed blood. I renounce all opportunities for ground held by Satan's wicked demons in relationship to this home and property. I ask You Lord Jesus to cast them from this home and all their controlling powers of darkness. I renounce all past use of this property for false religion, black magic and sorcery. I command the spirits of impurity, immorality, strife, jealousy, anger, selfishness and wickedness done by the people who lived on this property or in this home, to leave and never return in the name of Jesus. I declare wholeness, healing, salvation, prosperity and protection for everyone in this family, and all who enter this dwelling in the name of Jesus Christ, I pray, Amen.

Prayer for Restoration of Marriage:

Heavenly Father, Thank You for hearing my prayer, for I come to You in the name of Jesus and the authority of your Word. I come boldly to the throne of grace to receive mercy and find grace to help in restoring my marriage. I take my place standing in the gap for my husband/ wife against the devil until the salvation of God is manifested in their life. We forgive each other of any sins and transgressions. Help me Lord to remain pure and disciplined and to cherish my spouse. Deliver us Lord from the spirit of rejection and let us know we are accepted in the beloved. I come before You as humble as I know how, asking You Lord to heal this broken marriage as Jesus came to heal the brokenhearted. Lord, help us to submit to one another as we submit ourselves to you, in Jesus name we declare it done right now, Amen.

Prayer for Grieving the Loss of a Loved One:

Father please help _____ in their time of loss. Their/our lives are filled right now with grief, pain and heartache. But we turn our eyes to You as we seek Your strength, comfort and faithfulness. Lord, You are the God of comfort and love and I ask You to help them/us patiently wait on You. Help us through this pain and know that our hope is in You. I believe the promise in Your Word to send fresh mercy every day, and I trust that Your love will never fail me. Lord

Jesus, my/their heart is broken today, yet I know You can heal my/their sorrow. You are the Lord of mercy and the God of all comfort. I thank You, in Jesus' name, Amen.

Prayer for a Child:

Heavenly Father, please forgive me and every member of my family for our sins against You. Lord, help me to love others and do what You want me to do. Please take care of my loved ones and protect them always. Teach us always to come to You in prayer. Lord, help them to choose the right friends and that when they grow older they will accept you into their hearts and confess You as Savior with their lips. Lord, I ask You to give them a long, happy and healthy life and to teach them right from wrong. I ask You to give them favor with family, friends, teachers and classmates. Lord, You said in your Word, that You have never seen the righteous forsaken or their children begging bread. Help my children to know You better and to know that You are always with them. I love you and I praise you, in Jesus name, Amen.

Prayer for Commitment to the Will of God:

Heavenly Father, I come to You in the name of Jesus Christ. I renew and give my total allegiance to You Lord. Today and for the rest of my life, I will do all Your work in Your perfect will and will obey You at all times. I give my life and all that is in it, as a living sacrifice unto You, which is my spiritual act of worship. I will glorify You, honor You and bring praise unto Your holy name in all that I think, say and do. May Your total desire, will and Presence transform me into the likeness of Jesus Christ Your Son. I bind all of me, to all that You are, in Jesus' holy name, Amen.

Lord, Help Me Prayer:

Heavenly Father, help me not to be moved by the events happening around me. Help me to be moved by Your Spirit, Your Word and Your voice. Lord, I ask You to expand my territory and to increase me in the Holy Spirit and anoint me with Your power. I ask You to lead me in the paths of righteousness for Your name's sake. I ask You to release Your warring and ministering angels to minister on my behalf. Lord, remove in me, anything that is not of Your will and Your way. Shut any doors that need to be shut and open any doors that need to be opened. I plead the blood of Jesus Christ over me and my entire family, in Jesus name, Amen.

Prayer for Deliverance from Addictions:

Heavenly Father, I stand in faith on the authority I have as a believer in Jesus Christ. Your word says Satan has come down with great wrath knowing that he has only a short time. We know the thief comes only to steal, kill and destroy, but You have come that we might have life and have it more abundantly. In the name of Jesus Christ, I bind every evil and addicting spirit and every plan or scheme for my/their life. Help me/them to find strength in Your goodness and guidance. Almighty God, You sent Jesus to set the captives free and I know Your power and might. I ask You to deliver me/them from all addictions and bondages that have kept me/

them from being and doing my/their best. Help those around me/them to give sound and godly advice. You are my Deliverer, my Rock and my Fortress, my God in Whom I trust, in Jesus' name I consider this done, Amen.

Prayer for Financial Success:

Father, You said in Your Word, as I give, it will be given unto me, good measure, pressed down, shaken together and running over. You are able to make all grace abound toward me in every favor and earthly blessing, so that I have all sufficiency for all things in every good work. I am blessed in the city, blessed in the field, blessed coming in and blessed going out. You bless my lying down and my rising up. I confess I am blessed in the basket and blessed in my bank accounts, my investments, my health and my relationships are blessed and will flourish. May the blessings of the Lord overtake me in all areas of my life and I receive them in the name of Jesus Christ, Amen.[95]

About the Author

Rev. Dr. Michael Morawski is an ordained Pastor, Certified Chaplain, First-Responder and Adjunct Professor of Religious Studies at Central Connecticut State University. He is currently the New Member's Pastor, School of Ministry President and Head Ministerial Instructor at The First Cathedral, a multi-cultural church in Bloomfield, Connecticut which is the largest church in New England with over 11,000 members. "Pastor Mike" has a Doctor of Ministry Degree from Bethel Seminary in St. Paul, Minnesota where he majored in Church Leadership. He also holds a Master of Arts in Theology from Holy Apostles Seminary in Cromwell, Ct. and a Bachelor's Degree in Biblical Studies.

Pastor Mike has also written the book, *Dis-Grace: Immorality of Christian Leaders and How to Prevent It*.

Pastor Mike currently resides in Unionville, Connecticut with his wife Susan Morawski. Together they have 5 beautiful children and 7 grandchildren. Pastor Mike is available for seminars, lectures and counseling. Contact him at **pastormike@wordsofgrace.today**.

Endnotes

1. The Call - Os Guinness
2. Leading With A Limp - Dan B. Allender
3. Holman's Bible Dictionary
4. The Call - Os Guinness
5. Holman's Bible Dictionary
6. The Christian's Reasonable Service - Wilhelmus A. Brakel
7. The Making of a Leader - Frank Damazio
8. Preaching and Preachers - Martyn Lloyd Jones
9. Puritan Reformed Theological Seminary Guidelines - Joel Beeke
10. Ministerial Ethics and Etiquette - Nolan B. Harmon
11. ibid
12. Leader's Insight: Assessing Character - Angie Ward
13. Ministerial Ethics and Etiquette - Nolan B. Harmon
14. The Holiness of God - R. C. Sproul
15. The New Guidebook For Pastors - James W. Bryant and Mac Brunson
16. Zig Ziglar Quotes.com
17. Everyone Communicates, Few Connect - John Maxwell
18. Psychcentral.com - John M. Grohol
19. All Is Grace - Brennan Manning
20. Daring Greatly - Brene Brown
21. Anais Nin
22. The Great Doctrines of the Bible - Martyn Lloyd Jones
23. Christian Worker's Handbook - Billy Graham
24. The Four Spiritual Laws - Bill Bright
25. The Pastor's Handbook (NIV)
26. Evangelismcoach.org

27. The Broadman's Ministers Manual - Franklin M. Segler
28. ibid
29. ibid
30. The Pastor's Handbook (NIV)
31. The Handbook of Preaching and Worship - James Berkley
32. What Is Christian In Music? - Terry B. Ewell
33. The Pastor's Handbook (NIV)
34. How To Read Scripture Aloud - Lawrence W. Wilson
35. The Pastor's Handbook (NIV)
36. The Blessed Life - Robert Morris
37. The Broadman's Ministers Manual - Franklin M. Segler
38. Gotquestions.org
39. The Broadman's Ministers Manual - Franklin M. Segler
40. The Pastor's Handbook (NIV)
41. The Great Doctrines of the Bible - Martyn Lloyd Jones
42. The Baptism In The Holy Spirit - Derek Prince
43. ibid
44. The Seven Vital Steps To Receiving The Holy Spirit - Kenneth E. Hagin
45. The Baptism In The Holy Spirit - Derek Prince
46. The New Guidebook For Pastors - James W. Bryant and Mac Brunson
47. ibid
48. The Broadman's Ministers Manual - Franklin M. Segler
49. ibid
50. The Pastor's Handbook (NIV)
51. The New Guidebook For Pastors - James W. Bryant and Mac Brunson
52. Christian Worker's Handbook - Billy Graham
53. Getting Ready for Marriage Workbook - Jerry D. Hardin and Dianne C. Sloan
54. ibid

55. ibid
56. ibid
57. SaddlebackChurch.org
58. The Pastor's Handbook (NIV)
59. The Broadman's Ministers Manual - Franklin M. Segler
60. ibid
61. Idotaketwo.com
62. The Complete Book of Wedding Vows - Diane Warner
63. ibid
64. The Pastor's Handbook (NIV)
65. Christian Worker's Handbook - Billy Graham
66. ibid
67. The Broadman's Ministers Manual - Franklin M. Segler
68. Catholicworldreport.com
69. The Broadman's Ministers Manual - Franklin M. Segler
70. E.R. Wasemiller
71. The Pastor's Handbook (NIV)
72. The Broadman's Ministers Manual - Franklin M. Segler
73. The Pastor's Handbook (NIV)
74. ibid
75. Excerpts from Competent To Counsel - Jay Adams
76. Wayde I. Goodall, Ex. Dir. of Ministerial Enrichment, Springfield, MO.
77. Why Pastors Make Great Counselors - Robert Morgan
78. Larry Crabb uses a variation of these principles at his seminars.
79. Wayde I. Goodall, Ex. Dir. of Ministerial Enrichment, Springfield, MO.
80. The New Guidebook For Pastors - James W. Bryant and Mac Brunson
81. Counselors and Clergy: Partners in Healing - Stephanie Abbott, Douglas M. Ronsheim, Donna Xander
82. The Broadman's Ministers Manual - Franklin M. Segler

83. The Pastor's Handbook (NIV)
84. ibid
85. The Making of a Leader - J. Robert Clinton
86. The New Guidebook For Pastors - James W. Bryant and Mac Brunson
87. People Skills - Robert Bolton
88. Everyone Communicates, Few Connect - John Maxwell
89. Unknown
90. Dr. Frank Green
91. How to Develop and Cast Your Vision - Dr. Richard J. Krejcir
92. Christian Worker's Handbook - Billy Graham
93. The Pastor's Handbook (NIV)
94. Beth McLendon - inspirational-prayers.com
95. Christianword.org

NOTES

NOTES

www.ingramcontent.com/pod-product-compliance
Lightning Source LLC
Chambersburg PA
CBHW032249150426
43195CB00008BA/380